450

AFRICA AND
WORLD ORDER

AFRICA AND
WORLD ORDER

Edited by

NORMAN J. PADELFORD

and

RUPERT EMERSON

FREDERICK A. PRAEGER, *Publisher*

New York · London

Published in the United States of America in 1963 by
Frederick A. Praeger, Inc., Publisher
64 University Place, New York 3, N.Y.

Published in the United Kingdom in 1963 by
Frederick A. Praeger, Inc., Publisher
49 Great Ormond Street, London WC1

The essays in this volume originally appeared in a
special issue of *International Organization* entitled
"Africa and International Organization," Vol. XVI,
No. 2 (Spring, 1962).

Library of Congress Catalog Card Number: 63-10264

AFRICA AND WORLD ORDER is published in two editions:
A Praeger Paperback (P-111)
A clothbound edition

Printed in the United States of America

CONTENTS

21833

AFRICA AND
WORLD ORDER

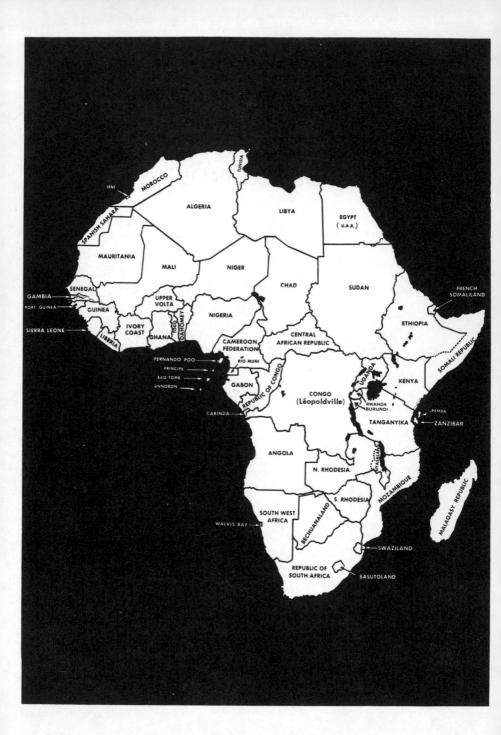

INTRODUCTION

The rapid transformation of Africa from an essentially colonial preserve of Europe to a region studded with more independent states than either Latin America, Western Europe, or Asia has been an unparalleled event in modern history. Appropriately, the years since 1955 have been termed by Africans "the decade of great change."

The significance for world politics in general and for international organization in particular of the emergence of African peoples to independence is incalculably great in many spheres and at many levels. It will be long before any definitive assessment can be made of events which are still tumultuously under way. Africa has only barely started to come to terms with its immense internal problems of all varieties, and with the need to work out its relations with the rest of the world. Independence, whether won through bitter struggle or handed over on a silver platter, poses hard problems. It begins, however, to be possible to sketch the shape and to sense the direction of some of the major forces and issues involved in the new Africa—and it is this that is attempted by the contributors to this book.

The mere matter of numbers gives a new urgency to a problem which the existence of twenty Latin American states had already made a matter of concern in the domain of international organization. With more than thirty African countries already members of the United Nations, and more to come, one can do little more than speculate as to the effect on international agencies of the multiplication of sovereign states, each entitled to its equal vote on all questions of peace and security. For the most part small in population, and meagerly endowed with the attributes that have customarily been regarded as rendering states important in international society, these states have already become the largest political grouping in the United Nations and in world politics. To pose an issue that reaches far beyond the themes treated in these pages, it seems inescapable that a fundamental rethinking must be undertaken of the structure of that organization, and of the role in it of the multitude of small nations, both new and old.

The Africans themselves have quite evidently not been happy, as at least two of the chapters in this volume indicate, with what they have come to call the Balkanization of their continent. Indeed, some among them see it as' another neocolonial device to perpetuate the substance of colonial rule through the manipulation of small, unviable states. What success will be achieved remains obscure, but there has been a constant coming and going

3

in the search for a means to realize the whole, or some first installment, of the Pan-African dream. A race is on between the widespread desire to find organized expression for African unity and the pressure of vested interests within each state to maintain separate independence, a status that includes, as one of its stellar attractions, sovereign participation in the United Nations and other international bodies.

The fruition of African nationalism has also brought a competition for power and influence within the continent. This has already been expressed not only in the vying of individual personalities, but also in the formation of several rival groupings—designated variously as the Monrovia, the Casablanca, the Brazzaville, and other groups—that are motivated by differing concepts of political association. The future of these kaleidoscopic associations is by no means clear. But it is apparent that their maneuvers have become a vital element in the international politics of this continent of new states. The competition for power and influence has also been manifested in the conflicting efforts to guide the course of events in the Congo toward certain preferred outcomes favored by external interests. It is evident, too, in the race to gain the energizing voice and hand in hastening the demise of the vestiges of European and antiblack rule in Africa. From these and other moves, one glimpses the initial configurations of an era of intracontinental politics unparalleled in African society. Will Africa turn toward peace and order, toward the fashioning of new and fruitful means of international collaboration? Or will it unwittingly slip into the pathways of conflict and war that led to so much pain and grief in the history of Europe and the Middle East? One can only hope amid doubts that it will be the former.

While the end of colonialism has entailed the disintegration of the international system imposed on so much of the globe by the imperial powers, all the links between the new states and their former rulers have by no means vanished. If the British Empire has dwindled to a pale shadow of its lusty past, the Commonwealth flourishes in a new guise and furnishes its own unique approach to international order and collaboration. South Africa has departed from it because of the racialism of its dominant Afrikaner minority, but other peoples of every color and creed have found in it a congenial fellowship. As for the French Community, the original assumption that it would be closely-knit and juridically organized seems to have been almost wholly abandoned. Intimate ties have been maintained, however, between France and most of its former African dependencies; the latter, in their turn, have become concerned to rebuild the ties among themselves. Here, too, the creation of a new system of relationships is more likely than not.

The most important focus of attention is, of course, neither continental nor ex-imperial, but the role of Africa in the world at large, particularly as reflected in the United Nations. In that organization, the issue of African nations is a question not only of quantitative but, markedly, of qualitative concern. What kind of United Nations will emerge from the influx of African members, the end of which is not yet in sight? With its vigorous caucus, the African contingent—excluding South Africa, which is set apart by its racist policies—can outweigh all other regional groupings at the U.N. And when united *en bloc* with the Asian states, this combination of powers can muster a near-majority of the total membership of the world body. This is a revolution never considered by the signers of the San Francisco Charter as a possible reality in the mid-twentieth century.

Given the preponderance of the Afro-Asian element, and the great weight of the growing body of African states by themselves, the entire character and alignment of the United Nations is undergoing drastic change. Every country, and perhaps most notably the United States, is confronted by the necessity to reappraise its views of the organization and of the part it can expect to play in relation to its national interest. The days when Washington could count on easy majorities for itself and its allies on any issue of consequence are in the remote past. The new United Nations is inevitably dominated by a passionate anticolonialism, by a demand for social and economic development, and by a neutralism whose manifestations may often seem capricious.

The essays that follow were originally written for a special issue of the quarterly *International Organization*, published by the World Peace Foundation. We are indebted to the Foundation for permission to incorporate in the present volume these searching analyses of Africa and its politics in relation to the United Nations.

Any discussion of Africa's place in the world order would be unthinkable without including the Africans' own concept of it. Yet where, amid the many voices of Africa, is there one that has so captured the span of the African political mind as to be able to reflect it in full? To give an idea of at least some of the facets of the African image of world order, we have turned to the podium of the United Nations, drawing from the words of Africa's own leaders and statesmen there the values they attach to participation in that organization. We realize, of course, that any selection drawn from the whole is incomplete, and that, for all that is outwardly expressed, much remains veiled or withheld. Still, in the policy statements of these leaders, we hear unmistakably authentic voices expressing at least some part of Africa's feelings and goals with respect to world order.

The emergence of Africa has had both a stimulating and a disruptive effect upon the United Nations. Great new spheres of activity have been opened to it, but there is as yet no clear evidence that the U.N. itself and the specialized agencies associated with it are capable of responding successfully to the overwhelming challenges being put to them. Nowhere have the poten-

tialities and the pitfalls of the new order of things been more starkly dis-
closed than in the Congo, which, while it certainly cannot be taken as typical
of all of Africa, represents some features of Africa in an exaggerated form—
indeed, as a shocking caricature of African hopes and fears. The African
peoples emerging from the colonial era pose a challenge to our international
society in almost every sphere. They need both world and African peace if
they are to advance; they should be protected from the intervention of the
great powers and helped to find their own place in the world; they need aid
and guidance to develop their economic, social, and political systems, still
only beginning the transition into modernity.

Emergent Africa is testing the strengths and weaknesses of the international order as they have not been tested before. The issues being raised are
of inescapable concern to all nations and people.

NORMAN J. PADELFORD
RUPERT EMERSON

Cambridge, Massachusetts
September, 1962

PAN-AFRICANISM

Rupert Emerson

The African scramble for independence has led to two major political trends which have at least the superficial look of being contradictory but which may still turn out to be complementary. One is the consolidation of states, and, it may be, of nations, within the frontiers traced on the map of Africa with an imperial flourish by the colonial powers. The other is the unceasing agitation and conferring to secure some sort of African unity which would bring together within a common framework either all the African peoples or such more limited groupings of them as are now prepared to join forces for general or particular purposes. The unanswered, and still unanswerable, question is whether the states which have been emerging in such quantities, with more still to come—29 African Members of the UN at the end of 1961 as against five in 1955—will serve as the building blocks for a greater African union or whether they will jealously guard the separate identity which they have now achieved.

The realist is likely to be tempted to dismiss Pan-Africanism as an idle and romantic dream, unable to make a significant breach in the solid walls of state sovereignty which Africans are in process of erecting. The turn of events may well prove him to be correct, but in the interim the devotion to Pan-Africanism is both widespread and charged with emotion. Nkrumah is far from being alone in his repeated insistence that the independence of particular African states takes on its full meaning only if all of Africa is free and if African unity is achieved. This sense of a mutuality of interest in freedom among all African peoples and countries found virtually no counterpart in the corresponding anticolonial drive of the Asian peoples, each of which pursued and enjoyed its independence without significant regard for the others. In the eyes of the believers the case for African unity rests not only on such utilitarian grounds as the need to collaborate and to establish a common front against Africa's enemies but also on the *mystique* of the conviction that Africans are born to share a common destiny. To the special circumstances of Africa which press toward unity the contention is often added that this is an era of global interdependence in which particularist nationalisms have become anachronistic.

I. Self-Determination and Territorial Integrity

The present consolidation of African states within the former colonial frontiers runs counter to much of what had been both predicted and desired during the colonial era. It was widely assumed that as soon as Africans came to freedom they would sweep aside the arbitrary boundaries imposed by the imperialists which cut across tribes and overrode the dictates of geography and economics. The continent had been partitioned to meet colonial convenience, but it would now be reshaped to realize its "natural" contours and return to its African essence. The accusation that the colonial powers had arbitrarily divided Africa among themselves rested on indisputable historical evidence; the further accusation, however, that they had broken up pre-existing African unity could be established only by a reconstruction of history. The balkanization of Africa is an old-established matter to which European colonialism only added new dimensions. Furthermore, the fact was normally neglected that while the job might on a number of counts have been much better done, the creation of states of a sensible size to live in the modern world could only be accomplished by a lumping together of tribal peoples who had no heritage of common identity.

The characteristic problem confronting anyone who seeks to establish the political shape of Africa south of the Sahara is that there are no "natural" communities or political entities between the smallest and the most typical expression of African community, the tribe, at one extreme, and the whole of the African continent at the other. A number of African kingdoms and empires which reached beyond a single tribe existed in the past, but they appear to have left only a slight imprint, if any, as far as a continuing sense of community is concerned, although the names of Ghana, Mali, and the like still command respect. Such regional groupings as West or East or Central Africa are not infrequently spoken of, but they generally lack clear definition, could be constituted in a number of different guises, and have no identifiable African past. This is not to deny that unions built on such regional foundations may come into being, but, only that, if they do, they will either be new creations or adaptations of cooperative arrangements established under colonial auspices.

The political vehicle to which the Africans south of the Sahara have everywhere entrusted their new found independence is the colonial state, despite the fact that none of these states had any existence prior to their invention by the colonial regimes responsible for them. (This includes Liberia if the Americo-Liberians are substituted for the colonial regime.) In all or most of the countries a great number of the people still have no effective awareness of their "national" stature, as defined by the colonial boundaries, but the political life of the leaders and their followers in the nationalistic movements was led at the level of the colonial territory. As soon as they got down to serious business parties and movements were organized on the basis of the several territories, and the immediate enemy to be overcome was the colonial government, even though at a remote distance behind it there stood the imperial power. During the search for independence each territory had its own party or parties, each concentrating on the political situation of that particular territory and paying relatively little attention to the activities of its neighbors. The one notable exception was in the two big French federations of West and Equatorial Africa, where parties—most notably the *Rassemblement Démocratique Africain* (RDA)—overflowed the lesser territorial boundaries and operated at a federal level in a number of the countries which have since come separately to sovereign independence. In the postwar years when the RDA flourished it was no doubt a relevant item not only that the federations were in existence but also that much of the political life of the territories centered in Paris and in the National Assembly where they were all represented, thus bringing the African leaders into intimate contact with each other. It seems reasonable to assume that the federal and Parisian ties which were thus built up among the leaders were largely responsible for the fact that since independence the former French colonies have made move after move to regain at least some of the unity which was sacrificed as the individual terrritories began to exercise the autonomy granted them under the *loi cadre* of 1956. In Lockean terms it might be said that the territorial units with which the leaders had mixed their political labor were the ones which retained political existence as colonialism came to an end; and in the French case this concerned both the twelve separate territories and the two federations they had constituted.

In most instances the transition from colonial status to independence was made in amicable agreement with the controlling power, which meant that the new African regimes could take over intact the going concerns, as they have been called, of the colonial administrations. Except for the lack of a foreign office and perhaps of a military establishment, the instrumentalities of government were already in operation and needed only to be nudged over to a new posture. The leading African political figures were often already substantially in charge of the affairs of their countries in the last phase of colonialism, and the africanization of the government services was in varying degrees under way. If new constitutions were generally written, they tended to build on the inherited institutions. The more painful transition in the case of Guinea, where France resented the assertion of independence, and the speedy disintegration of the Congo, where no preparation had been made for independence, only underlined the good fortune of the rest.

The universal African acceptance of the practice of concentrating on the going concerns of the inherited colonial territories had worked to undermine the earlier conviction that major re-alignments of the political boundaries would be necessary. This earlier version found expression in one of the resolutions of the first All-African People's Conference which met in Accra in December 1958. Speaking up for the unity of Africa and a Commonwealth of Free African States, this resolution

> denounces artificial frontiers drawn by imperialist powers to divide the peoples of Africa, particularly those which cut across ethnic groups and divide people of the same stock; calls for the abolition or adjustment of such frontiers at an early date; calls upon the independent states of Africa to support a permanent solution to this problem founded upon the wishes of the people.

This doctrine appears to find continued expression in some of the statements and policies of President Nkrumah, in part no doubt as justification for his claim that because of tribal affiliation Togo and parts of the Ivory Coast should be joined to Ghana. Their "liberation" would be a part of the process of doing away with colonialism's evils—although Sylvanus Olympio of Togo and Félix Houphouet-Boigny of the Ivory Coast fail to see it in that light.

A significant reaffirmation of Nkrumah's position appeared in the communiqué which he and President Abdulla Osman of Somalia issued at the conclusion of the latter's visit to Ghana in October 1961. It will be remembered that Somalia has extensive territorial claims against Ethiopia, Kenya, and French Somaliland, based on the Somalis on the wrong side of the frontiers. The communiqué sees a union of African states as the step which would automatically make obsolete the frontier problems inherited from the colonial regimes, but also recognizes the imperative need to call upon the principle of self-determination as a means of removing the artificial colonial frontiers which were drawn without respect for ethnic, cultural, or economic links.[1]

This is not a doctrine which has found favor as the years have gone by.

---

[1] *The Party* (Accra), October 1961 (No. 14), p. 13. When it was reported that Sylvanus Olympio, then Prime Minister of Togoland, was opposed to the integration of his country with Ghana, the Ghanaian Ministry of Foreign Affairs issued the following statement: "The arbitrary carving out of the African Continent by the imperialist powers during the 'scramble for Africa' in the 19th century resulted in an unnatural and unsatisfactory situation. People of the same ethnic group, indeed sometimes members of the same family, came to be ruled by different powers and were compelled to regard their brothers across the border as foreigners. The Ewes along the Ghana/Togoland border are not the only such victims. The Sanwi, Aowin and Nzema peoples on the Western borders of Ghana are in a similar plight.

"The Prime Minister's suggestion is therefore no bid for expansionism. It represents the natural urge of these peoples to achieve the basic ethnic regrouping of the communities which had been violated by the plans of the imperialist powers for domination and exploitation." *Ghana Today* (London), November 25, 1959.

Indeed, as early as April 1958, the Conference of Independent African States, also meeting at Accra, in demanding respect for the independence, sovereignty, and territorial integrity of African states, took a conservative position very difficult to reconcile with the revolutionary implications of self-determination. Be it noted that this was a conference of *states,* and not of *peoples,* the latter term meaning parties, movements, and other non-governmental organizations. I have been able to find in the records of the several succeeding African conferences of either states or peoples no repetition of the plea that self-determination should be relied upon to restore Africa to its proper dimensions. The more left-inclined gathering of African states at Casablanca in January 1961 seems to have made no pronouncement on these subjects, except, of course, its call for African unity, but the larger meeting of twenty African states at Monrovia in May 1961 came out firmly for the absolute equality of states, noninterference in internal affairs, respect for sovereignty, and unqualified condemnation of outside subversive action by neighboring states. In this setting self-determination is acceptable only for territories as a whole and not for ethnic pieces of them.

Responsible political leaders everywhere are wary of the principle of self-determination, and African political leaders have good reason to be warier than most. For the reasons which have been suggested above, the African state system as a whole and in its parts is fragile. It has neither the sanction of old-established political entities nor well-knit communities to lend stability to its states. The effective units of community are the tribes, but to open the door to African tribal self-determination would be to move toward a balkanization which would verge on anarchy, if it did not wholly achieve it. Furthermore, it is generally true that the present leaders seek a modernization of their societies in which the tribal past would play at best only a ceremonial role. To allow the tribes to take over as the dominant elements in the shaping of Africa would be to expose to ruin much of what these leaders have accomplished and seek to accomplish in the immediate future. The tragic affairs of the Congo, where tribalism partially reasserted itself when the central authority collapsed, stand as a warning as to what may happen.

Given the circumstances of Africa it is eminently comprehensible that there should be a determination on the part of many African statesmen to stand by the existing political structure of the continent even though any one can with ease poke his fingers through the loopholes with which it is riddled. The consolidation and utilization of what presently exists seems a far sounder procedure than an effort to reconstruct the political map of Africa which would run the immediate risk of creating a far worse situation than the one which now exists.

Considerations of this sort led President Olympio to look with a skeptical

eye on the pretensions of Pan-Africanism and to plead the cause of the
present African countries:

> In their struggle against the colonial powers the new African states, arbitrary and
> unrealistic as their original boundaries may have been, managed at last to mobilize
> the will of their citizens toward the attainment of national independence. Achieved
> at great sacrifice, such a reward is not to be cast away lightly; nor should the
> national will, once unified, be diluted by the formation of nebulous political units.[2]

It is a fair summary of his contention to say that he warned against pursuing a shadowy vision of African unity and counseled instead the use of
the tools at hand to tackle "the central task to which we are committed—
the earliest possible economic and social betterment of our people." For
this purpose, he held, the principle of national sovereignty should be retained, combined with an active policy of cooperation with other African
states.

In similar vein the Abbé Fulbert Youlou, President of the Congo
(Brazzaville), is cited as having remarked concerning Pan-Africanism that
"those who talk about it should start by sweeping up in front of their own
hut, before thinking of sweeping up before that of their neighbor."[3]

II. The Sources of Pan-Africanism

The Pan-Africanism which is being pursued simultaneously with the
internal consolidation of the new states has many faces and can take on
many guises. The simplest and, all in all, perhaps the most satisfactory
version of it is the sense that all Africans have a spiritual affinity with each
other and that, having suffered together in the past, they must march together into a new and brighter future. In its fullest realization this would
involve the creation of "an African leviathan in the form of a political
organisation or association of states," as Nnamdi Azikiwe, Governor-
General of Nigeria and one of the pioneer leaders of African nationalism,
recently put it in a speech in which he expressed his conviction that such
a leviathan was bound to arise.[4] At lesser levels it might involve an almost
infinite variety of regional groupings and collaborative arrangements, all
partial embodiments of the continent-embracing unity which is the dream
of the true Pan-Africanist.[5]

---

[2] Sylvanus E. Olympio, "African Problems and the Cold War," *Foreign Affairs*, October 1961
(Vol. 40, No. 1), p. 51.

[3] Cited by E. Milcent, "Forces et idées-forces en Afrique Occidentale," *Afrique Documents*, Mai
1960 (No. 51), p. 63.

[4] Nnamdi Azikiwe, "The Future of Pan-Africanism," a speech made in London on August 12,
1961, published by the Nigerian High Commission, London.

[5] The article by Erasmus H. Kloman, Jr., which appears elsewhere in this issue, gives an account of
many of the more recent African groupings.

The sources from which Pan-Africanism derives are in part obscure and debatable and in part reasonably clearly written on the record.

How much of the claimed sense of common identity is to be attributed to the feeling that all Africans, despite the unmistakable physical differences among them, are members of the same race? Here, as in most other social-political manifestations of the idea of race, what is important is not the unascertainable biological fact of common physical heritage but the belief that there is such a heritage, at least in the sense of distinguishing Africans from the other peoples of the world.

One complication raised by the racial approach is the question as to whether North Africa, Arab and Berber in composition as against the *Afrique noire* south of the Sahara, forms a part of a single continental Pan-Africa. If blackness of skin be taken as the principal outward criterion of Africanness, the North African peoples evidently belong in a different category, but the general assumption and practice have been to include North Africa in the Pan-African family, despite the fact that it has attachments to the Arab world of the Middle East not shared by sub-Saharan Africans as well as attachments to the broader world of Islam which are shared by only some of the peoples to the south. My own crystal ball suggests that while for some purposes the North African countries will be drawn into continental African groupings, they will continue to have Arabic, Mediterranean, and Muslim affiliations which will keep them from anything approaching total absorption into a conceivable Pan-African union.

Even though Africans generally, having been the principal victims of a prior racialism, repudiate a new racialism asserting itself in a Pan-African guise, it seems very difficult to escape racial conceptions as one of the basic elements in Pan-Africanism. The concept of *Négritude,* expounded by Aimé Césaire, Léopold Senghor, and others, bases itself explicitly on the people of "Negro race" (incidentally leading into the further demographic question as to the relation of African-descended people through the world to a Pan-African or Pan-Negro movement). Nkrumah's conception of the African Personality is less obviously tied to racial moorings but it cannot evade the racialist implications which are inherent in any such idea. Senghor overtly brings these implications to the fore in his assertion that

Négritude is the whole complex of civilised values—cultural, economic, social, and political—which characterize the black peoples, or, more precisely the Negro-African world. . . . the sense of communion, the gift of myth-making, the gift of rhythm, such are the essential elements of Négritude, which you will find indelibly stamped on all the works and activities of the black man.[6]

It is both fruitless and unwise to seek to give to either *Négritude* or Afri-

[6] Léopold Sédar Senghor, *West Africa,* November 4, 1961, p. 1211.

can Personality a precise and specific content. Both, like Americanism and other similar concepts, stand as proud symbols of the accomplishments and virtues of a people, to be phrased in large and generous terms. Any effort to define them more closely runs the risk of starting arguments which divide those whom it is sought to unite rather than to bring them together. One key feature of these concepts and of the general trend of African think- ing in recent years is that black has become a color to admire and be proud of. The earlier assumption, convenient for the slave owner and white ruler, had been that white represented the superior beings endowed with a high and advanced civilization whereas black stood for the properly servile in- feriors who had not progressed beyond the primitive stages of mankind. African nationalism has brought about a transvaluation of values which es- tablishes the African as a person of consequence and the heir of a history and culture, still in process of rediscovery, which have made their contribu- tion to the world. To be black is itself a distinctive bond of unity.

Running through this range of thought and emotion is the conviction that the Africans as a people have been oppressed, exploited, and degraded to a greater extent than any other great mass of mankind in history. No elaborate exposition of the centuries of the slave trade, slavery, and colonial- ism is needed to point the moral of the African belief that they have been collectively mistreated and that their common identity has been forged in the flames of their common suffering. If all hands have been against them in the past, it is all the more necessary for them now to join forces to ensure that their weakness does not again invite disaster.

In the creation of the conception that the continent forms a single Pan- African whole a large role has been played by the Negroes overseas and particularly those in the West Indies and the United States. Having lost the memory of the particular tribes and regions from which they came and being aware of the anonymous unity which slavery had thrust upon them, it was natural that they should look across the Atlantic and see Africa and their fellow Negro brethren as a whole. Many Negro religious figures, teachers, professional men, and others contributed to the stream which flowed toward Pan-Africanism, but four names can be singled out as pecu- liarly significant: E. W. Blyden, who was the distiguished nineteenth cen- tury precursor of later developments; W. E. B. Du Bois, who fathered a series of Pan-African Congresses; Marcus Garvey, who sought to establish a "universal confraternity" and a "central nation" for the Negro race; and George Padmore, who served as a crystallizing center for Pan-Africanism in London, influencing many Africans, including Kwame Nkrumah.

The considerable number of African leaders who have been educated or have lived abroad must have experienced a similar inclination toward a Pan-African outlook as they were thrown into contact with Africans from many countries and were forced to look at the affairs of their continent through other eyes and from afar.

It seems eminently probable that not only Africa's elements of unity but, perversely, its diversity and heterogeneity as well have had an influence in promoting Pan-Africanism. Precisely the instability of African states within their arbitrary frontiers and the lack of any "natural" stopping points between the tribe and continental Africa in the large lend an attraction to the broader view which it might not otherwise have—and which it may cease to have if and when African states achieve the internal consolidation which they are now seeking. The depth and breadth of an exclusive attachment to the new states is inevitably open to question, and it is reasonable to think that some of the ills from which Africa suffers or which potentially threaten it can be better handled on a collective basis than by some forty separate political entities. Thus Gabriel d'Arboussier, Senegalese Minister of Justice, predicting a Union of West African States by 1965, sees as the decisive weapon in the present evolution of Africa the unity which it has not yet achieved but which is imposed on it by its multiple diversities and internal divisions whether they be tribal, religious, ethnic, or territorial.[1]

In particular, the threat of contingent anarchy contained in the fact that Africa's tribal structure only accidentally coincides with state frontiers might be greatly eased if larger unions of states could be brought into being, thus making possible arrangements by which tribes that straddle boundaries within the union could reestablish some measure of unity. It is, of course, true that in many parts of Africa boundaries are sufficiently porous to enable people to move easily back and forth across them in the interior, but the more states assert their sovereignty the more the boundaries will seal them off from each other, making formal agreements necessary if tribal and other customary links are to be maintained. Thus an East African union, for example, of the kind which has been much discussed recently, could lay the groundwork for a solution or at least an amelioration of the three-way political partition which has been imposed on the Somalis and the Masai and perhaps of the problem of the Kenya coastal strip as well.

III. The Varieties of Pan-Africanism

To identify the sources of Pan-Africanism is a far easier task than to predict what practical results it is likely to achieve.

The first goal which the Pan-Africanists have always set for themselves—the liberation of all of Africa from alien rule—should be reached shortly with the one great exception of South Africa where the end of white domi-

[1] Gabriel d'Arboussier, "La coopération des Etats africains et les problèmes internationaux," *Afrique Documents*, Mars-Avril 1961 (No. 56), p. 68.

nation in the peculiarly objectionable form of *apartheid* is still not in sight. The two other major areas of difficulty are the Rhodesias with their strong white minorities and the Portuguese territories of Angola and Mozambique where no effective move has been made to prepare the Africans to manage their own affairs. Failure to achieve speedy independence and self-government for the African majorities in the great southern reaches of the continent would be a blow to African aspirations, but it is arguable that nothing could better promote the practical advance of Pan-Africanism than its confrontation by a continued unyielding colonialism, perhaps involving new Sharpevilles in the form of violent suppression of nationalist agitation. The result of such a situation might well be that Africa's independent states would band more closely together to furnish aid to their oppressed brethren than they would otherwise be ready to do.

The first step is to win independence; the second is to knit together the newly freed peoples. On the face of it, there is a ring of gross improbability about the dream that within the foreseeable future a great leviathan might be created which would embrace all the African states within a single political structure. Although some sort of collaborative functional arrangements may conceivably be worked out on an Africa-wide basis, it is likely that any close political union will be limited to regions such as West or East Africa, and that even at the regional level functional collaboration, as, for example, in relation to transport and communications, health and sanitary provisions, and certain economic matters, is much more probable than a merging of sovereignties. Furthermore, any strong regional movement or organization would be likely to impair the possibility of realizing a full Pan-Africanism. Thus, the meeting of the Pan-African Freedom Movement of East and Central Africa (PAFMECA) in Addis Ababa in February 1962, which seems to have broadened and strengthened the ties among East and Central African countries and to have added some South African connections as well, was viewed with dismay by Ghanaian observers who saw it as threat to all-African solutions.

One important federation which seems sure to break up is the Federation of Rhodesia and Nyasaland which has been bitterly fought by the African communities, particularly in Northern Rhodesia and Nyasaland, since its origin in 1953. As African majorities take over in these countries the hostility to the links which bind them to Southern Rhodesia will presumably make the maintenance of the existing federal structure impossible although a new scheme of African-inspired organization may emerge, perhaps within the broader framework offered by PAFMECA. The Commission for Technical Co-operation in Africa South of the Sahara (CCTA) is also running into difficulty because of the continued membership of the colonial powers, and most notably of the Portuguese.

To the regionalism of geography may be added two other categories of regionalism: one of language and the other of ideology.

A regionalism of language finds its principal expression in the efforts of the former French dependencies to regain some of the advantages which came to them as members of the West and Equatorial African federations and to build even more extensive joint enterprises within the ranks of the African peoples *d'expression française*. The most elaborate of these is the so-called Brazzaville group, or, more formally, the Union of African and Malagasy States, which has a membership of a round dozen of the former French colonies and trusteeships, only Guinea, Mali, and Togo having held aloof from it. After several earlier meetings, at one of which the subsidiary Organization for Economic Cooperation was created, the conference at Tananarive in September 1961 further elaborated the structure of the union, adopting an over-all charter, establishing a Post and Telecommunications Union, and drawing up a defense pact which requires ratification by the parliaments of the members. Two lesser groupings embrace four of the states formerly in French West Africa and the four which made up Equatorial Africa.[8] The continued existence of these organizations within the Union is specifically provided for, as is the participation of the Union in the arrangements deriving from the Monrovia conference.

No corresponding links have been formed among the former British African territories, although those which have come to independence have remained within the Commonwealth—and remained all the more happily with the departure of South Africa from it. It is, of course, also true that in maintaining the Federation of Nigeria the British held within a single political unit approximately as many people as were contained in the whole of French Africa south of the Sahara.

At least until very recently English-speaking Africans and Negroes tended to monopolize both the term "Pan-Africanism" and the movements and congresses associated with it.[9] In part, perhaps, this arose from the fact that many of the outstanding French African leaders were for a time drawn to France and to Paris, with the result that they somewhat lost sight of

[8] The multiplicity of the groupings which can appear was well illustrated by the speech made by President Youlou in welcoming the heads of state of former French Equatorial Africa to a conference in Brazzaville in November 1960. Asserting that this was the hour of communities, he ended with a *vive* for each of the four republics, the Equatorial Community, the African Community, and the Community of States *d'expression française*. No grouping having an African language as its base has yet been seriously proposed.

[9] "As a movement which was conceived in America and which blossomed in West Africa, pan-Africanism remains essentially an English-speaking movement, a delayed boomerang from the era of slavery as practiced on the West African coast two centuries ago. It is significant that, linguistically and ethnically, most of the American Negroes in North America came from the coastal areas on the Gulf of Guinea, and only a few from the interior areas of Senegal and Niger." Paul-Marc Henry, "Pan-Africanism: A Dream Come True," *Foreign Affairs*, April 1959, p. 445. See also T. Hodgkin and R. Schachter, "French-speaking West Africa in Transition," *International Conciliation*, May 1960, p. 432; Philippe Decraene, *Le Panafricanisme*, Paris, 1959.

their African heritage. It has also been suggested that France frowned
upon Pan-African conceptions because their advocates were likely to be
precisely those radical nationalists who were pressing most vigorously for
modernization and equality: "French repudiation of the goal of independence led to deep suspicion of the goal of unity."[10] Whether or not the French
are to be held directly responsible for the breaking up of the federations of
West and Equatorial Africa, it is clear that they did nothing to encourage
their maintenance or re-establishment after 1956.

As independence came in sight, however, French-speaking Africans have
demonstrated an increasing interest in associating themselves with the Pan-
African movements from which they have at all events never been wholly
divorced. Particularly for those who, like Senghor, stressed the anachronistic parochialism of nationalism in the contemporary world, the broader
horizons of Pan-Africa were inevitably appealing, and even the union of
Africa was seen as only a steppingstone to the union of mankind.

Another side of the coin is the accusation which has been leveled by
Nkrumah and others against the ex-French states that they are tools of
neocolonialism both in allowing the language barriers imposed by imperialism to determine their alignments and in the degree to which they have
remained tied to France financially and otherwise. Certainly a number
of the territories left behind in the collapse of the two federations seem
hopeless experiments in endowing with life artificial political entities which
have no prospecrt of economic and political viability. Their dependence on
France for the barest minimum of survival cannot help but raise questions
as to the reality of their independence; and for the entire Brazzaville group
it is a plausible speculation that a large share of such coordination as they
have achieved between themselves has been the product of activities which
have taken place in Paris rather than in one or another African capital.

IV. Casablanca and Monrovia

The two major ideological groupings, which go under the names of the
cities in which they originated in 1961, Casablanca and Monrovia, both cut
across the linguistic boundaries and thus help to prevent a permanent freez-
ing of the lines dividing the former British and French territories. On a
larger scale these two groupings carry on the attack on linguistic solidarity
which was initiated with the Ghana-Guinea union in 1958, later extended
by the addition of Mali (the ex-French Soudan) after the breakup of the
Mali Federation in 1960.

Although it is tempting to read a deep and long-lasting ideological con-

[10] Immanuel Wallerstein, *Africa: The Politics of Independence*, New York, Vintage Books, 1961,
p. 111.

flict into the split between these two major groups, many observers are inclined to be skeptical of the solidarity of each of the groups within itself and of the depth and sticking power of the ideological divergence. Certainly it is premature to assume that any political situation in Africa has as yet had time to achieve real stability. Both within each of the states and in the relations between them forces are at work which sharply challenge the existing order and may end by overthrowing it. The series of apparently cordial state visits which the heads of countries in the opposing blocs pay each other, with the consequent communiqués endorsing friendship and African unity, indicate that the ideological lines are far from representing any total separation.

When these cautionary remarks have been made, however, it is essential to recognize that as of now serious cleavages divide the members of the two groups which tend to head in different directions in outlook and policy. Undoubtedly the Casablanca group, of which Guinea, Ghana, and Mali constitute the sub-Saharan members, is more activist, radical, and left-oriented, taking its anticolonialism, its socialism, and its Pan-Africanism a good deal more seriously than does the larger and more conservative Monrovia grouping in which Nigeria and Liberia play leading roles and which includes the entire Brazzaville community as well as Ethiopia and Somalia from the other side of the continent. Relations between Guinea, Ghana, and Mali on one side and the Soviet bloc on the other tend to be considerably more intimate than those between the latter and the Monrovia contingent.

As a matter of principle it is possible to find a sharp differentiation in the Monrovian tendency to look to a series of agreements on functional collaboration as contrasted with Nkrumah's constant insistence, laid out for example in his opening address to the first All-African People's Conference in 1958, that the primary aim must be the attainment of the Political Kingdom, after which all else will follow."[11] In practice, however, neither the Guinea-Ghana-Mali union nor the Casablanca group as a whole has made any significant move toward an actual political merger, although the constitutions of the first three countries provide that sovereignty can be surrendered in whole or in part in the interests of African unity. One concrete success which Nkrumah has achieved was the agreement with President Yameogo of Upper Volta in mid-1961 to remove the customs barriers between the two states, a step which Nkrumah hailed as wiping out the artificial territorial barriers imposed by the imperialists. On its side, the Monrovia group, in its meeting at Lagos in January 1962, adopted in principle

---

[11] John Marcum distinguishes between the Casablanca and the Monrovia groupings on the basis of their representing monolithic and pluralist unity respectively. "How Wide is the Gap between Casablanca and Monrovia?" *Africa Report*, January 1962 (Vol. 7, No. 1). This article contains (p. 4) a useful table showing the membership of African countries in the different groupings.

a charter for African unity which would bring an elaborately structured organization of African states into being.

The Nkrumah doctrine that African unity must be sought through a merger of sovereignties in a new Political Kingdom has not found many takers among the African leaders. The reasons for this rejection are not hard to find, among them being the manifest disinclination to accept the proferred headship of Nkrumah himself in a potential African union. This is a difficulty which must be a recurrent one: where strong one-man leadership has established itself, as is so often the case in Africa, it will be a painful process to select from among the leaders of the states which are uniting one to stand out in splendor while the others sink back to subordinate positions. The surrender of the trappings and the more substantial perquisites of sovereignty is not a step which is lightly taken, even for the attainment of African unity. Several of the African leaders have indicated plainly enough that they have not fought the battles for independence in order to abandon it again in favor of someone else's rule. Thus the Prime Minister of Nigeria, with an icy side reference to Nkrumah, remarked that his country had waited one hundred years for freedom and did not propose to throw it away on gaining independence, and Houphouet-Boigny similarly protested that his Ivory Coast had not come to independence in order to be subjected to a backward African country.[12]

V. African Harmony and Discord

Deep in the heart of every true believer is the conviction that the principle of the natural harmony of interests applies in his domain. For the Pan-Africanist this implies belief in the assumption that, once the affairs of the continent cease to be distorted by the machinations of the colonialist and neocolonialist, African states and peoples will live in harmony with each other. Such a view rests upon the faith that the apparent differences and difficulties between states can be overcome by goodwill since all Africans have common outlooks and desire the unity of their peoples. In actuality the potentialities for conflict among African states are as great as those in other parts of the world; and several of them center on Ghana

[12] For Nkrumah, see *The New York Times,* January 14, 1960. For Houphouet-Boigny, see "Les Chances de l'Afrique," *Revue Politique et Parlementaire,* Juillet 1961, p. 3–11. Nnamdi Azikiwe in 1959 affirmed his confidence in the creation of the United States of Africa, but warned that:

> It would be capital folly to assume that hard-bargaining politicians who passed through the ordeal of victimization and the crucible of persecution to win their independence will easily surrender their newly-won power in the interest of a political leviathan which is populated by people who are alien to one another in their social and economic relations. It has not been possible in Europe or America, and unless Africa can show herself different from other continents, the verdict of history on this score will remain unchallenged and unaltered.

Zik, A Selection from the Speeches of Nnamdi Azikiwe, Cambridge, University Press, 1961, p. 72.

either because of its ethnic-territorial claims on Togo and the Ivory Coast or because of plots which it is alleged to have concocted against the regimes in other African countries. Three other disputes may be mentioned which seem symptomatic of the kind of troubles which may be coming along as the African states work out their relationships among themselves and establish their own continental balance of power: Morocco's claim to take over Mauritania, the demand of Somalia that the Somali-inhabited portions of Ethiopia and Kenya should be joined to it, and the controversy between Cameroun and Nigeria as to the status of the northern portion of the former British Cameroons. To these must of course be added any number of possible disputes arising from cross-frontier tribal claims, not to mention all the usual subjects which offer fertile fields for disagreement among states.

The suspicions which divide the African states came out clearly in the opening address of Governor-General Azikiwe to the conference of the twenty Monrovia group countries at Lagos on January 25, 1962. Referring with regret to the absence of the Casablanca contingent (it was, incidentally, rumored that Guinea and Mali would have liked to attend), he warned about an ideological difference between the two groups which stemmed from "the conspicuous absence of specific declaration" by the Casablanca states of belief in the fundamental principles enunciated at Monrovia. These were the inalienable right of African states, as at present constituted, to legal equality, to self-determination, to inviolability of their territories from external aggression, and "to safety from internal interference in their internal affairs through subversive activities engineered by supposedly friendly states." He recalled that the United Nations Charter provides such safeguards in general terms, but asked for overt adherence to the Monrovia principles.

> Otherwise it can be a matter for speculation whether these principles are capable of becoming spectres to haunt the conscience of those who would rather pay lip service to the Charter of the United Nations, whilst secretly they nurse expansionist ambitions against their smaller and perhaps weaker neighbors.

Another variant of difference between the African states, this time coming from the Casablanca side, was contained in a speech delivered by President Modibo Keita of Mali in June 1961.[18] Here he spoke of his continuing conviction that the countries of Africa can never achieve full independence as long as they remain small and each concentrates on itself alone. Although, he pointed out, the constitution of Mali provides for total or partial abandonment of sovereignty on behalf of a grouping of African states, actual political unification with other states could be undertaken only if there

[18] Modibo Keita, "The Foreign Policy of Mali," *International Affairs*, October 1961, p. 435–6.

were an identity of views on both international policy and domestic economic policy. Even without such an identity of views, cooperation would
be possible with all African states, whatever their political or economic
position, but the conditions for a political merger were much more strin-
gent. President Keita had, of course, been one of the central figures in the
collapse of the Mali Federation, whose demise could in good part be attributed to sharp disagreements on both foreign and domestic policy between Senegal and Soudan. It might be added that the more recent divorce
of Syria from Egypt, shattering the United Arab Republic, was in part
attributable to similar differences in outlook and policy between the two
countries.

Which way the African future will turn is still a matter for wide-open
speculation. It is evident that strong forces are pulling in a number of
different directions, that African states are frequently divided among themselves, and that all African leaders express their devotion to the cause of
African unity although with varying interpretations and varying degrees of
intensity. Most of them would undoubtedly concur in the verdict of Julius
Nyerere, principal architect of Tanganyika's independence, that African
nationalism is different from other nationalisms of the past in that "the
African national State is an instrument for the unification of Africa, and
not for dividing Africa, that African nationalism is meaningless, is dangerous, is anachronistic if it is not at the same time pan-Africanism."[14]

How different African nationalism is remains to be seen. Insofar as
precedents are relevant it is clear on the historical record that elsewhere
the more parochial nationalist forces have almost always won out over the
more broadly integrating supernational forces. It remains the fact that the
rediscovery of Africa by the Africans is still only in its opening stages.
It is a vast continent which has always been internally divided, and the
superimposed colonial divisions worked to prevent the different peoples
from establishing any real contact with each other. Pan-African gatherings, United Nations caucuses, and a host of other meetings and interstate
visits are bringing at least an upper crust of the African peoples in touch
with each other, but it will be long before the colonially-determined lines
of transport and communications can be so reconstructed as to open up easy
intercourse between the countries.

But perhaps the precedents are not relevant. Times have changed and
African nations still have an insubstantiality about them which distinguishes them from their fellows around the globe. Of all the questions
which may be asked the most significant is as to the depth and universality
of the belief that Africans are born to a common destiny.

[14] *World Assembly of Youth Forum,* No. 40, September 1961, p. 14. Most of the leaders would
presumably also agree with Nyerere's further contention that only African unity can save the continent
from the rival imperialisms of capitalism and communism.

THE IMPACT ON THE COMMONWEALTH OF THE EMERGENCE OF AFRICA

John Holmes

When Africa emerged with unexpected haste as an independent political force in the world, the Commonwealth was still adjusting itself to revolutionary transformations in Asia. There was no doubt that it had entered on a new phase, but the phase was hard to define. Because the nature of the Commonwealth is implicit, there is always considerable diversity of view on its significance even among its own citizens. There is always a time lag as well. Many people, particularly in the "Old Commonwealth," had just begun to grasp the significance of "The Commonwealth," no longer "The British Commonwealth," no longer a blood relationship; and now they had to cope with its rapid expansion and the imminent prospect that white members would be in a minority. Neither citizens nor foreigners had even made up their minds whether they were viewing the decline and fall of the British Empire or the finest hour of the Commonwealth. The doctrine that the new multiracial Commonwealth was the blessed culmination of the virtues of the Empire, the triumph of its good instincts over its errors, had certainly become the official view celebrated in speeches and communiqués, but public opinion lagged behind—not so much resistant to the new idea as captive of traditional attitudes. Not only the white people's view was anachronistic; Asians and Africans were themselves slow to recognize and accept their new position of equality and of responsibility.

The impact of emergent Africa on the Commonwealth, therefore, has been unsettling and stimulating, not in itself revolutionary because the revolution had already taken place. Africa has confirmed the revolution, given the Commonwealth a new sense of mission, and injected into it a needed dose of ebullient African vitality. At the same time, of course, it has raised—or restated—questions about the continued existence of this unique historical phenomenon.

I. Changing Attitudes

The Commonwealth has always developed by adjusting to circumstances and concocting its theory retroactively. The British Commonwealth of

JOHN HOLMES is President of the Canadian Institute of International Affairs. He was for some time in the Canadian Foreign Service. During preparation of this article Mr. Holmes was attending the Commonwealth Relations Conference in Lagos, Nigeria.

white dominions, which lasted until the Second World War, evolved out of the voluntary adjustment in the relationship between Britain and Canada to permit equality and independence compatible with a political tie. When in 1947 India and Pakistan, somewhat unexpectedly, indicated a will to remain in the Commonwealth, the practical advantages of thus extending membership were apparent to most members, and they were prepared to adjust the theory as needed. Only the perspicacious saw at the time how far this path would lead in transforming and de-Briticizing the Commonwealth or accepted the implications of the shift in the balance of power in Commonwealth councils. When the Africans came along, however, the extent of the revolution was made obvious.

One consequence of the new Commonwealth precipitated by the emergence of Africa is that it now engenders more enthusiasm left of Center and somewhat less to the right; and in the noncommunist world it is widely regarded as a "progressive" rather than a "reactionary" force. Although there is still strong support for the Commonwealth in the British Conservative Party, right-wingers like the Marquis of Salisbury, a dedicated Secretary of State for the Dominions when they were all white, now rejects the Commonwealth for the more congenial white man's club of Europe. Within the Labour Party there are now probably more true believers than in the Conservative Party. In official Commonwealth councils the liberal wing, led by Canada (whether its government was Liberal or Conservative) has been reinforced as against the more imperially-minded Australians. Canadians in general find more enthusiasm for the multiracial Commonwealth than for the purely British kinship which for half their citizens was unnatural. Whereas in the past Canada had emphasized the prior importance of resisting centralizing tendencies, more recently it has exerted its influence to strengthen and put more meaning into a Commonwealth which, Canada has come to realize, has considerable diplomatic value for a middle power. The old Canadian principle of stressing Commonwealth consultation but avoiding any prior commitment to a common policy has not been abandoned but glorified, because it is the only basis on which Asians and Africans would consider membership at all. There are fewer Canadian inhibitions, however, about assuming leadership and responsibility in making the Commonwealth a diplomatic force to be reckoned with.

The assertiveness of India, Canada, and Australia, over the past decade and a half meant that the Commonwealth has become less Anglocentric—a phenomenon not yet adequately appreciated outside Commonwealth chanceries. Britain has remained the center if not the formal capital, the clearing-house, the performer of residual jobs, the organizer of agenda, and of course the tutor for aspiring members. However, as other members grow in diplomatic resources, the significance of London as fount declines—although it remains very much *primus inter pares*. In the United Nations and elsewhere members have developed their own relationships with each other, shared views and information, and worked together in causes sometimes at odds with the views of the United Kingdom—a notable example being the teamwork of India, Pakistan, and Canada to rescue the British from the Suez crisis. This trend is already being accentuated by the emergence of Ghana and Nigeria in international diplomacy.

II. Decline of Traditional Imperial Relationships

As formal links have declined in significance, increasing emphasis has been placed on consultation as the virtue and advantage of the Commonwealth association. The inevitable declarations of satisfaction over "free and frank discussion" on set occasions may sound hollow at times, but there is in fact profit for all in the constant contact of European, Asian, and African thinking, and the diplomacy of all members has reflected the exposure to each other's views. A sense of solidarity was stimulated during the formative period of the New Commonwealth in the early 'fifties by something approaching a consensus among India, the United Kingdom, Canada, and New Zealand on the handling of China and the Chinese periphery in Korea and Indo-China—a consensus which differed basically in approach from that of the United States. This consensus has, of course, been sorely strained by differences within the Commonwealth between the nonaligned and the aligned, between the anticolonists and the members of NATO and SEATO—and yet it is this clash of attitudes which gives Commonwealth consultation its significance.

The role of the monarchy had been settled before the Africans came along. It was accepted in 1949 that a republic could remain a member, and thereafter the monarch could no longer be counted on as the constitutional center of its being. The Queen remains symbolically "Head of the Commonwealth," however, and her position in the Commonwealth may have been strengthened by the acceptance of republicanism where it is natural. As her visits to India and Ghana have demonstrated, she inspires a respect and an affection that might have been prejudiced if her throne had remained a symbol of domination over "British subjects" rather than a symbol of respect for "Commonwealth citizens." Africans seem to have a fondness for queens, and although their states will probably become republics, the person of the monarch may play a more significant role than had been expected in maintaining the Commonwealth emotion.

As the tie of common political attitudes has been increasingly emphasized, two traditional imperial values have been declining in significance— the military and the economic.

Visions of "imperial defense" lingered until the Second World War. Even after the war Britain had world-wide commitments to defend, and the Suez Canal still seemed the link with the Eastern empire. The lesson of the war, however, was that Britain's reliable link with Australia and New Zealand was the Panama Canal and the defense of those countries conceivable only in concert with the United States. Withdrawal from direct responsibility for the defense of India and the retreat from Suez finally disintegrated the concept of the Commonwealth as a unity for defense. This change was for a time masked by the growing British partnership with the United States in a policy of containing communism and the creation of the Baghdad Pact and SEATO as a very thin anti-red line around the world. It is this purpose and the protection of oil and other interests in the Middle East rather than the traditional defense of empire which has perpetuated British interest in far-flung bases. Aden and Singapore have been maintained, and new military establishments created in Cyprus and East Africa. However, the pressure of military requirements in Europe and of economics, as well as disillusion about the advantages of a world mission, are leading influential military thinkers in London to contemplate withdrawing from all commitments no longer related to the specific needs of the home country. About all that remains of the conception of imperial defense is a fraternity of Commonwealth armed services based on traditions, and mutual aid for training purposes. Not all the assistance is now being given by Britain, however; Canada, for example, has supplied the Ghanaians on request with a training mission.

This revolution in British military thinking is of importance for Africa. Anxiety to preserve the military base in Kenya is not likely to interfere with that country's progress to self-government. When the Nigerians recently asked to terminate their defense agreement with the United Kingdom, this was arranged with a minimum of ill will and regret. Older members of the Commonwealth are concerned about the threat to Africa of communism, but they think of it in political and economic terms rather than military. It seems likely, therefore, that Africa's emergence will complete the demilitarization of the Commonwealth as an organization—if not of its individual members. At the same time it has strengthened the philosophy of nonalignment within the circle. It is a misjudgment to consider the Commonwealth a "neutralist" association, but it is also a misjudgment to think of it now as an instrument of "the West." Its function is conciliation rather than "hot" or "cold" war.

The old imperial economic structure has likewise been decomposing as new members have diversified their commerce and turned to the United States and other countries for aid and investment. Commonwealth preferences have steadily declined in importance in the past twenty years, and the sterling area and the Colombo Plan are no longer coterminous with the political limits of the Commonwealth. Nevertheless, habits and channels of trade and investment remain, and the tendency to minimize the present importance of Commonwealth economics has been interrupted by the storm which has blown up over Britain's proposed entry into the European Economic Community (EEC). Even Canada, for which Commonwealth trade has been less significant than for any other member, has placed an unexpected value on Commonwealth preferences; the Asian members have insisted upon the importance of the British economy for them; and the situation has revealed the desperate dependence on British markets and investment of the African members. At the recent meeting of the Commonwealth Finance Ministers in Accra a unanimous and angry united front emerged against Britain over its entry into EEC. There is, however, an assumption in these arguments that the present problem is not one of perpetuating a Commonwealth economic system, of which there are few advocates, but one of helping member states over a difficult transition either to a new system of regional economic blocs or to a revived multilateralism.

III. The Commonwealth and Colonialism

The emergence of Africa has also affected the Commonwealth's conception of itself.

The first African country to become a full Commonwealth member was Ghana, and it played a significant role in confirming and extending the new conception of the Commonwealth. As each Asian member had joined the circle, old ideas of imperial rule retreated further. India, Ceylon, Malaya, however, were countries of ancient culture, entities for whom self-government had long been envisioned, however dimly. As the Gold Coast grew restless, it was inevitable that the new pattern of Commonwealth would be seen by both sides as the solution, even though the path to self-government had hitherto been viewed as a much more gradual process in Africa. It was welcomed not only as an answer to the immediate problem of how to cope with nationalism in the Gold Coast but also as the formula to solve the major British dilemma of the age—how to cast off the burden of empire in a manner satisfactory to British investments, prestige, and conscience. This formula for Africa was by no means as obvious ten or even five years ago as it now seems in retrospect.

This solution, furthermore, set the pattern for other empires and for the United Nations. For the British it was much easier to cope with the Trusteeship Council and anticolonial pressures in the Assembly because of the established pattern of Commonwealth development which, as experience proved, would lead to unfettered independence. The anticolonialists complained of the pace, but, whether they admitted it or not, they accepted the Commonwealth precedent as the model for all Africa. And the Gold Coast was the bright star—a shining example which accounts for some of the present bitterness over its deviation from Commonwealth political conceptions. When the Gold Coast became Ghana and entered the United Nations, Krishna Menon praised British colonial policy. Because the world in general and the Africans in particular had confidence in British intentions, it was even possible, as in the case of Nigeria and the West Indies, to slow down the precipitation into self-government in order to prepare the domestic scene for the shock of independence. By setting a hot pace, however, the British confounded the French and spurred the Belgians into tragic haste. They have also exposed the untenable position of the white settlers in eastern and southern Africa and driven them toward crisis. So far, the African period has been good for the prestige and morale of the whole Commonwealth and has stimulated in Africans a pride in the institutions which they have helped to create. More difficult problems, however, are yet to be faced, and the Commonwealth itself might well be shattered by differences over the processes of liquidating colonialism in East and Central Africa—not to mention Angola and the Republic of South Africa.

The arrival at the Commonwealth table of Ghana, followed by Nigeria, Sierra Leone, and Tanganyika, with others to come, made the Commonwealth genuinely multiracial and intercontinental, strengthening thereby its role, now more than ever emphasized, as a bridge between East and West and North and South, a fraternity which links regions and blocs in an enterprise in mutual understanding. It added a continent and another dimension, a new force within the Commonwealth to help relieve old tensions. The whole structure became grander, more significant, and at the same time more flexible.

IV. Changing Balance of Power Within the Commonwealth

The application of the Commonwealth principle to Africa led to the transformation of the institution in another important sense. It forced the acceptance of a Commonwealth unlimited in numbers. Previously, it had been taken for granted that the Commonwealth, to maintain its peculiar virtue, had to remain intimate. There was much to be said for this assumption. It is hard to avoid the conclusion, however, that the thinking of Whitehall was dominated by its conception of the Commonwealth as something which had to fit the cabinet room at No. 10 Downing Street. For years the prime ministers had assembled for their more or less regular meetings in this hallowed place, but the Ceylonese got just about the last seat in the house. It had long been arguable that the more important aspect of a prime ministers' meeting was the bilateral confabulation in hotel rooms and the group photograph with the Queen on the infinite lawns at Windsor. There was reason to doubt whether the prime ministers' meetings were sufficiently important in the Commonwealth scheme of things to play such a decisive role in determining its character. Nevertheless, the view persisted that the only way to cope with the crowd was to give the smaller applicants observer status. With Sierra Leone and Cyprus specifically in mind, the British initiated Commonwealth consideration of a two-tiered Commonwealth. It was sceptically received, and even Mr. Macmillan recognized that it was hard to define two categories of membership when the obligations of membership as they stood were indefinable and intangible. The whole idea of a limited membership, however, was blown away by the rush of applicants from Africa—assisted, perhaps, by the acquiring for Commonwealth purposes in London of more spacious quarters.

Although there was uneasiness about the implications of this multiplication of non-European members on the balance of power in the Commonwealth, there was no firm resistance. Rather there was an acceptance of the view that this risk was more than compensated for by the broadening of the scope and influence of the Commonwealth. The Commonwealth has never been governed by majority votes. Insofar as it reaches any decisions, it does so by consensus. Such decisions in any case are normally concerned only with its own constitution and ritual. It rarely tries to speak with one voice on world issues, except in general terms, as in the declaration of the prime ministers on disarmament in March 1961. Even in the decision on South Africa there was no vote. A consensus was reached in accordance with the way the winds were blowing. In such circumstances, therefore, the fear of being outnumbered is less precise.

This is not to say, however, that there have not been profound effects on the Commonwealth of the shift of balance. The nature of the consensus is bound to be different as the non-European voices swell. Its stock of political ideas now incorporates as much of Gandhi as of Balfour, and is dominated by themes of nonviolence or racial harmony rather than of cabinet government. Already this change has had its impact on one of the basic principles of the earlier Commonwealth, the principle of noninterference in each other's domestic affairs.

The withdrawal of South Africa in 1961 has changed the Commonwealth, and that action is directly attributable to the arrival of the other African members. It was not only the states present at the prime ministers' meeting in 1961 but also the prospective members who forced the departure of South Africa. When Mr. Nyerere warned that Tanganyika would reconsider its position in the Commonwealth if South African policies were condoned, he put at stake that continuing progress of dependent territories

to Commonwealth status which had become the chief glory and justification of the institution. It was the Africans who swung the balance. Mr.
Nehru, already the elder statesman of the Commonwealth, was not pressing for expulsion, for he belonged to the generation which cherished the
principles of independence and noninterference. But those principles had
now been taken for granted and the new generation of leaders, even a conservative like Tunku Abdul Rahman of Malaya, was more concerned with
asserting the political principles that the Commonwealth, to justify itself,
must hold self-evident.

V. Significance of the South African Issue

In the South Africa question two ways of looking at the Commonwealth
were at issue. There is the traditional conception of the institution as a
kind of family, a family of mixed blood but nevertheless a family in that
it has no reason for existence except that it shares a common origin. It is
not a club but an historical phenomenon. Countries do not join it; they
are born into it. As in a family, it is not necessary to subscribe to a set of
beliefs, but there are family traditions to be honored. Prodigals were not,
heretofore, cast out but suffered to remain so that they might be regener-
ated by the influence of a good home. It is not a tightly knit family at all.
Each member has religious, political, and other associations which often
have priority over family ties, but nevertheless there remains the unique
family association. Until 1961, the family traditions were assumed to be
concerned mainly with a common belief in principles of goverment and
law similar in spirit if not necessarily in form to those of Westminster.
The traditional rules of the Commonwealth were also implicit; it was
understood that members did not bring judgment against each other's domestic policy. South Africa and India, India and Pakistan could quarrel
over issues of race or boundary, and Canada and New Zealand could quarrel over butter, but no member would seek a Commonwealth decision in
its favor. Against these traditional attitudes, however, was the increasing
insistence of new members that adherence to the more recent principle of
racial equality took precedence over the preservation of the family. These
attitudes were not, of course, doctrinal in inspiration; those who argued
against South Africa might very well argue for noninterference in a different set of circumstances.

The earlier assumption had been that the Commonwealth was a company of saints and sinners, none spotless, and that the practice of the principles, whether of free government or nondiscrimination, would in no cases
be impeccable. Pakistan had not been thrown out for failing to achieve
parliamentary government, but Pakistan had not turned its back on free

THE IMPACT OF AFRICA ON THE COMMONWEALTH 31

institutions of government as a goal. In the case of South Africa, the government had disavowed the intention of ever recognizing racial equality, something quite different from the lapses in performance of other members. No member had, heretofore, been expelled or even censured by the Commonwealth as an institution, although members had criticized each other in and out of the United Nations. The offense of South Africa posed an issue which could not be ignored as the tendency grew to justify the very existence of the Commonwealth by its nonracialism. Most of the prime ministers were aware of the implications of driving South Africa out, but they did so because they realized that there was no alternative if the Commonwealth was to be preserved at all.

What has been gained is that in the new African states there is a pride in the Commonwealth which could not otherwise have existed. What is lost is the more flexible relationship of the past. Among older members, furthermore, there is a sense of having failed over South Africa, the accession of which to the Commonwealth after the Boer War had given the institution much of its original inspiration and impetus. There remains in influential quarters in the "Old Commonwealth" a discontent over these events which has diminished enthusiasm for the whole institution. An important cause of this discontent is the belief that the new members, now in the majority, place more importance on the assertion of racial equality than on the principles of free government. There is fear also that once the hypothesis that a member can be judged for offending against Commonwealth principles has been accepted, no member is immune from the hostility of a majority. The particular object of concern is Ghana, as the question is asked whether Mr. Nkrumah may not abandon what would be considered a minimum Commonwealth faith in free institutions and escape censure because he is not white. It is feared that since there is now a non-European majority, non-European members will not be subjected to impartial judgment. This possibility does exist, but it is questionable whether one should assume that members of the Commonwealth will cease to act with their customary restraint and respect for each other. Even the action against South Africa, far from being vindictive, was taken only after Mr. Verwoerd had been conceded every opportunity to avoid this consequence.

VI. The Commonwealth and African Regionalism

Paradoxically, the new African members, although they are as jealous of their independence as Canada ever was, may reverse the long prejudice against common action. They are impatient with the metaphysics of the Commonwealth which have long fascinated the more constitutionally-minded older members. Having insisted that the Commonwealth should believe in something tangible and should take action, they are likely to press for more tangible benefits from the association. At the unofficial Commonwealth Relations Conference in Lagos in January 1962, when older members began contemplating with habitual satisfaction the virtues of consultation and the blessed paradoxes on which the institution thrives, a Nigerian pointed out that consultation might have been the principal benefit for older members (and at this conference India and Pakistan were clearly in the role of "Old Commonwealth"), but the Africans were looking for more than that. What they want is cooperative assistance. They have no intention of making the Commonwealth for them an exclusive association; Pan-Africanism, as Julius Nyerere has recently made clear, is bound to take precedence. Nevertheless, they are searching for ways in which the Commonwealth—which brings them contact not only with other continents but also with each other, scattered and divided as they have always been—can help them in the causes dearest to their hearts, economic and social development and African unity.

Indicative of this kind of thinking was the interest at the conference in a Commonwealth initiative in setting up a "Colombo Plan for Africa"— a "Lagos Plan," it was suggested. Like the Colombo Plan, it would be the product of Commonwealth initiative but broadened for the benefit of others—not a "Plan for Commonwealth Africa" but a "Commonwealth Plan for Africa," as one African speaker put it. They have no desire to limit African economic programs to the Commonwealth, but in grasping for a framework in which to get started working together they recollect the administrative unity under the imperial regime which Nigeria, Ghana, and Sierra Leone once had in the west and which Uganda, Kenya, and Tanganyika have retained in the east. Among these former colonies there are associations based on language, education, habits, and political attitudes which provide at least a rudimentary basis for cooperation in a fragmented continent woefully lacking in communications.

Of vital importance to the Commonwealth is, of course, the development of regionalism both in Africa and in Europe.

The European Economic Community is regarded by the Commonwealth states of Africa with disquiet. They see in it a sinister move of the Europeans, under the suspect leadership of France, to reassert their power, to reimpose through the mechanism of the status of "Associated Overseas Territories" their domination over Africa, and to keep them producing cheap raw materials for European industry. Their objections to EEC are more political than economic and they tend to view British entry into the Market not only as a disaster for their economies but also as an act of betrayal. In spite of their castigations about British imperialism, there is in Africa an expectation from the former ruler not only of economic aid but also of special consideration and political affection. If they are jilted by the British in favor of the Europeans in whom they have little trust they might leave the Commonwealth in dudgeon. There is some speculation as to whether the Commonwealth without Britain might survive with Indian and Canadian leadership, but it is hard to take this conjecture seriously. African interest in other parts of the Commonwealth is growing, and in time the association within the Commonwealth of the African-Asian majority might develop a validity of its own, but it is still too new and tentative to compensate for the more tangible links the Africans have long had with London and Oxford, Birmingham and Edinburgh.

At the Lagos Conference the Africans recognized that the future of Pan-Africanism also raised questions about the future of the Commonwealth. All members, it was agreed, had regional or special ties loose enough to be compatible with the Commonwealth association—ties with NATO or SEATO, the "Bandung Powers" or those which Trinidad, Jamaica, or Canada might form with the Organization of American States. Associations of this kind left participants free to determine their own national policies. However, if Britain were to lose its freedom of action in European union or if the African members were to lose theirs in a federal Africa, then it was doubtful if these members could play any meaningful part in the Commonwealth. The wisest advice on this subject came from a prominent Nigerian who said that it was inadvisable to look too far ahead. For the present the Commonwealth was valuable and should be maintained. If in the progress of history the patterns of states changed, then the role of the Commonwealth could be re-examined. It was quite likely, he thought, that the adaptable Commonwealth might even then find grounds for its continuing existence, but there was no point trying to solve that question until the circumstances were known.

It is healthy for members of the Commonwealth to recognize that the institution they cherish will not last forever and that its disappearance may be the proof of its success rather than of its failure. It has already proved itself to be one of the higher forms of political organization, but history sweeps all political organizations into evolution. The worthiest function of the Commonwealth has been as a formula and a framework to aid in the transition of empire. This process of transition is the most perilous phenomenon of our age, and the fact that the transformation of the greatest of modern empires has so far been accomplished with a minimum of violence and an unprecedented amount of goodwill is cause for the whole world to be gratified. The Commonwealth is already certain of its place as a noble chapter in history—provided, of course, that history is not written exclusively by doctrinaires of the Right or the Left.

The period of transition, however, is not over yet in Africa, and there is still a vital function for the Commonwealth. Its continued existence is not predetermined, subject to the inexorable law of history. Its continuance is a matter of will, and for the time being that will seems to exist, for various reasons, in Africa. In all countries of the Commonwealth, however, and particularly in the older ones, it is advisable to see it in its historical perspective in order to repress anachronistic urges to recreate it as an exclusive organization and in order to stifle the illusion that it is a feasible economic or political unit. The Commonwealth association must be regarded as complementary. It is not an alternative to regional organization or world organization. It should not be an obstacle to progress but a catalyst. Its unique strength is that it has sought to promote unity by enlarging understanding rather than to induce unity by imposing constitutional strait jackets. As such, it is a healthy influence at a time when we are in danger of losing sight of the fact that the promotion of unity within regions does not serve the cause of world order if it exaggerates disunity between regions.

AFRICA SPEAKS TO THE UNITED NATIONS

A Symposium of Aspirations and Concerns Voiced by Representative Leaders at the UN

No consideration of the place of Africa in the United Nations or of the role of international organization in the progress of this continent would be thinkable without an authoritative expression of views upon the subject by Africans themselves.

Unlike some parts of the world, Africa does not speak with one voice or through one spokesman. Out of its newly found freedom the aspirations, the concerns, and the determinations of its people and their leaders are spoken instead through many tongues and with varying intonations and outlooks. What is felt in one country or group of countries to be the proper touch or approach is not always shared by others. Yet as one listens to the representatives of the now 30 African states at the United Nations, and as one watches their conferences and actions, it becomes apparent that they do share many common aspirations, ambitions, and intentions. The intensities of these and the emphases given to them differ considerably. Plotted along a spectrum there are substantial distances separating some of them. These reflect in part some of the group attachments which are mentioned in the chapter by Mr. Kloman. In part they bespeak ideological and political leanings.

In view of these considerations, it has seemed best to us to let heads of states or official delegates from various parts of Africa speak through their own words what they expect of the United Nations, how they view the future of Africa in the Organization, what their deepest concerns are as they face the "decade of development," and what they demand of others. Their statements are taken from the general debate at the fifteenth and sixteenth sessions of the General Assembly.

We are aware, of course, that a selection of excerpts is at best just that; and that in extracting these views we have had to leave out many others. For the full import of what these leaders have said, and for the no less important statements of other heads of state or ambassadors whom we have had to pass by here due to the limitations of space, we refer the reader to the *Official Records* of the General Assembly.

We trust that this brief symposium will nonetheless give an appreciation of the thinking of Africa upon some of the vital issues of international organization in our day. The statements have been arranged generally according to the order of admission of the countries to the United Nations.

THE EDITORS

Katema Yifru

Acting Minister of State of Ethiopia[1]

. . . As a small country, Ethiopia has always known that the greatest measure of protection and the most effective safeguards against breaches of the peace, aggression, and the abuse and disregard of the rights of small nations are to be found in this Organization. . . .

On world problems we start from the premise that no nation today wants or seeks war. . . .

At the same time we cannot shrug off the plain fact that the two Great Powers today are following policies which, quite apart from their inherent rightness or wrongness, must and do inevitably lead them into conflict and friction. To the extent that these conflicts arise from the efforts of either group to secure acceptance of its particular political or economic philosophy, or in an attempt to impose their system of government upon others, we here at the United Nations not only have the right but the duty to insist that they stay their hands lest miscalculation occur and destroy us all. . . .

Though it can be said that we must be realistic, that we must recognize the limited nature of our ability to prevail upon the Great Powers to stay their hands from the nuclear trigger, we can nevertheless unanimously demand an immediate halt to all nuclear tests, followed by a complete nuclear ban . . .

Disarmament has become for our time the overwhelming imperative. In no other area, perhaps, has so much been said and so little accomplished. The Ethiopian delegation believes that we should do more on the question of disarmament.

. . . we can challenge [the Great Powers] . . . to make a firm commitment in advance to abide by the decisions which this body may reach, and thus test the sincerity of the protestations which ring in our ears—though often punctuated by the explosions of nuclear devices—that both sides desire peace.

High on the list of topics, and clamoring for our attention, is the final liquidation of colonialism. . . .

We can settle for no less and will be satisfied with nothing else.

. . . every dependent African territory must be free. . . .

We . . . call upon the government of the United Kingdom to grant the right of equal suffrage to the African population, so that each territory may determine its own future no matter what the desire of the settlers might be.

. . . The only policy that is realistic and acceptable to Africans is the transfer of power to Africans. . . .

The case of Angola cries out for special consideration . . . enough is

[1] Sixteenth Session, A/PV.1020, October 2, 1961.

known to demand our immediate intervention and to elicit our universal condemnation. . . .

A scarcely less compelling problem exists in the policies of racial discrimination which continue to be followed in certain states. . . . we look principally to the Union of South Africa, where a legalized policy of discrimination exists. In our view, the United Nations has done far too little in the past with respect to this problem. We therefore call on all Member States to join in collective action, in sanctions which will demonstrate to South Africa once and for all that the way of life which it has professed is repugnant to mankind and that, considerations of principle aside, it is not in the interests of that country to follow it any longer.

The numerous violations of the terms of the mandate held by South Africa over South West Africa have been taken jointly by Liberia and Ethiopia to the International Court of Justice at The Hague. This action will be pressed with full vigor and energy. We are happy to report that all the African states have participated in all decisions leading to this action [and] . . . that Ghana and other states are planning to intervene before the Court in support of this action. We feel that this cooperation augurs concerted action in other areas of common interest. The Court action, however, is not enough. We call, therefore, for a greater measure of action than has been taken in the past and one which will provide for tangible and positive results. . . .

Last year, by an overwhelming vote, the General Assembly called for the speedy dissolution of the last strongholds of colonialism. Unhappily, this resolution has remained largely unimplemented. . . . Let us act now, forthrightly and honestly, to dispel this problem and to remove it permanently from the agenda of this body.

. . . the spread of the Cold War . . . constitutes a particular danger for Africans and Asians . . . threatening thereby the peaceful and rational development of their economic and social structures. . . . We believe it to be essential to provide the institutional framework whereby problems which are essentially local in nature are limited to the locality most intimately concerned. In order to achieve this end for the continent of Africa, we call upon our sister states in Africa to join in the creation, under Article 52 of the United Nations Charter, of a regional organization of African states, the basic and fundamental task of which will be to furnish the mechanism whereby problems which arise on the continent and which are of primary interest to the region could, in the first instance, be dealt [with] by Africans, in an African forum, free from outside influence and pressure. . . . our desire is not to disengage ourselves from the world community, but to develop institutions peculiar to ourselves in accordance with the Charter.

. . . Because of our belief in the peaceful coexistence of nations irrespec-

tive of differences in political and social systems, and because of our realization of the advantages emanating from the universality of the United
Nations membership, the Ethiopian delegation will support the proposal
that the government of the People's Republic of China occupy its rightful
place in the United Nations.

. . . there must be an increase in the membership of both the Security
Council and the Economic and Social Council to facilitate an increased
participation by the Afro-Asian states which are at present poorly represented.

Regarding . . . the Secretariat . . . it is appropriate that one person occupy
the post of Secretary-General. In fairness to all concerned, it is preferable
to select as a Secretary-General a national from the Afro-Asian countries.

. . . It is imperative that the closest advisers to the Secretary-General
should also be staffed on the basis of equitable geographical distribution.

. . . Our experience in the Economic and Social Council has convinced
us more than ever that the interest of the underdeveloped countries can
best be served by channeling all aid and assistance through the United Nations. The problem in the social and technical assistance activities of the
United Nations is not only one of making available more funds to the Organization. Undoubtedly, the increase of such funds is indeed imperative,
but there is also the problem of effectively utilizing the available resources.

J. Rudolph Grimes
Secretary of State of Liberia[2]

. . . Quite recently there have been complaints about the manner in which
some decisions [of the United Nations] have been executed. . . .

Distrust of a particular personality who may occupy the position of Secretary-General or disagreement with the manner in which a Secretary-General
may implement a resolution should not constitute a motive to destroy or
undermine the office of Secretary-General.

Indeed, should this attitude persist, it could conceivably reach a stage of
absurdity in which each year, as our national policies change and as we
desire to use the instruments of the United Nations to pursue our national
objectives, we would find ourselves demanding not merely a change in the
person of the Secretary-General but also in the institution. The office of
the Secretary-General should not be used to further the policy or interest
of any particular country.

My government will not support any proposal designed to emasculate the
position of the Secretary-General by introducing three persons representing
socialist states, neutralist states, and Western states, nor any proposal for

[2] Sixteenth Session, A/PV.1017, September 27, 1961.

three Deputy Secretaries-General representing such blocs, who are to be concerned with political, diplomatic, and *ad hoc* functions.

In the first instance, apart from the fact that there are some Members of the United Nations who will continue to pursue an independent policy without being connected with any one of the three mentioned blocs, we do not and will not approve a permanent division of the Members of the United Nations into blocs, which would have the effect of rigidifying a division not only not contemplated by the Charter but also absolutely contrary to its provisions.

Only an amendment of the Charter could change the position of the Secretary-General; but such a change is undesirable because it would paralyze the Organization and set up criteria of such a transient and evanescent nature that it would be impossible of exactness, and this would be contrary to the principles and purposes of the Organization. . . .

In spite of our obligations as loyal members of this lofty Organization we are confronted with situations in which some Members of the United Nations—some of them even permanent members of the Security Council—either deliberately ignore decisions of this Organization themselves or encourage other states to do so.

When a matter is decided by the Security Council by a majority vote and a permanent member abstains, it is unfair for such a member to refuse to carry out the decision of the Council since it had the opportunity both of preventing the decision of the Security Council and of having the matter referred to the General Assembly.

. . . There cannot be a double standard. The yardstick by which the measurement is taken must be the same for all Members of the United Nations.

But what has been even more shocking is the apparent desire of some states—again some of which are permanent members of the Security Council—to attempt to wreck the Organization through financial strangulation by refusing to contribute to its peacekeeping activities. . . .

It is wrong for any Member of the United Nations to refuse to make its contribution on any ground whatsoever; for when either the Security Council or the General Assembly takes an action it does so on behalf of each Member, and we are all obligated because we have conferred on these institutions the power to take action on our behalf. . . .

But the problem becomes even worse when one or more permanent members of the Security Council refuse to contribute to the peacekeeping activities of the United Nations, for it demonstrates thereby a shameful disregard of the solemn obligations which it has undertaken in the discharge of its duties. One wonders whether a country which acts in such a manner is really worthy of permanent membership of the Security Council. It may well be that the whole concept on which the Security Council of the United Nations was created should be re-examined, for we cannot be sure that important duties should be entrusted to such Members.

My delegation feels that peacekeeping operations of the United Nations are an obligation of Members and, therefore, the expenses thereof should be apportioned by the General Assembly in keeping with Article 17 (2). . . .

The various councils and other organs of the United Nations have usually been established by elections under some arrangements in which seats were allocated to certain geographic areas. Under the present arrangements, Africa has not generally been included in these geographic allocations. No one needs to be told that it is unfair to constitute these organs in a manner which excludes representation of approximately 25 percent of the entire membership of the Organization. We have urged repeatedly that these organs should be enlarged to permit the election and participation of African states. . . . The only legitimate alternative is a rearrangement of the existing seats so that Africa can be represented by each of them. It is fervently hoped, therefore, that other Members of the United Nations will support one or other of these alternatives in order to give greater participation to African states. . . .

One of the purposes of the United Nations is to achieve international co-operation in solving international problems of economic, social, cultural, or humanitarian character, and I submit that this is both a pressing and an explosive problem. A great cooperative movement or organization must be undertaken to help in developing the much needed skills, providing the capital, and planning a massive assault on poverty, ignorance, hunger, and disease. Bilateral and multilateral approaches are necessary because of the magnitude of the task.

It is here in the United Nations that the developed countries should increase their contributions to technical assistance, the Special Fund for Economic Development, and like organizations to enable them to do more in finding an effective solution to this problem. . . .

The Portuguese government [has] defiantly refused to permit the United Nations Commission to enter Angola to [inquire into the situation in Angola]. . . .

A dangerous practice seems to be developing on the part of some countries of ignoring decisions taken by this Organization, and we have to be careful not to tolerate it or to permit it to go unchallenged. It is hoped that the commission will make a full report. It is reported that arms allegedly supplied by NATO to Portugal are being used to carry out these repressive measures. NATO countries contend that arms supplied for defense are not provided for such military purposes, but the fact remains that some of those self-same arms are being used to repress the legitimate aspirations of the indigenous people. My delegation will therefore propose at this session that an arms embargo be imposed against Portugal. . . .

The problem of the mandated territory of South West Africa is one which has been before the General Assembly from the very beginning. Even though many resolutions have been passed, it is regrettable that nothing has been achieved . . . the mandate itself has been violated in several respects. . . .

The situation in South Africa itself, where *apartheid* is being rigidly applied to such an extent that it led to the dreadful Sharpeville shootings in 1960, has not improved in spite of the Security Council's resolution. This problem which goes to the heart of proper relations among people on the basis of equality and infringes human dignity, perhaps in its most insidious form, continues to threaten international peace. The powder keg in that area will not remain hidden without explosion which could have a serious effect in the world. . . .

Ibrahim Abboud

President of the Republic of the Sudan[a]

. . . Nineteen hundred and sixty was fittingly called "the year of Africa" because of the impressive number of new nations from that continent admitted to membership of the United Nations during its fifteenth session. But Africa will also always remember the sixteenth session as the first session in the life of the Organization to have been presided over by a devoted son of Africa. . . .

My country has been a Member of this Organization for six years now; and reviewing the records of the United Nations in these six years I note that many vital problems of international life have become perennial items on the agenda of successive sessions. . . . Numerous resolutions are passed only to be repeated at the following session. I must confess that we are disappointed at this state of affairs. . . .

At the top of the list of the problems the continuance of which pose a real and grave threat to international peace and security is the problem of disarmament. . . . The United Nations, we maintain, should play the leading role in this field. . . . What the General Assembly should now stress is the inescapable necessity of general and complete disarmament and the immediate cessation of nuclear and thermonuclear tests. . . .

To explode nuclear devices on one's own territory is reprehensible enough; and to do the same on the territory and at the doorsteps of others is morally, as well as legally, wrong.

May I from this rostrum solemnly renew the appeals to the governments

[a] Sixteenth Session, A/PV.1036, October 13, 1961.

of France, the Soviet Union, and the United States to suspend, forthwith, these tests in order to facilitate an early resumption of negotiations aiming at an agreement on the question of general and complete disarmament. . . .

We are unshakably of the conviction that one of the main causes of the ominous tensions engulfing the world today and posing a direct threat to international peace and security is the continued existence of colonialism, in its classical or modern forms, in many parts of the world. This conviction was endorsed by the overwhelming majority of this Organization when it adopted, on 14 December of last year, Resolution 1514 (XV) relating to the granting of independence to all colonial countries and peoples.

In spite of this unambiguous injunction from this august body, it is sad to note that colonial wars of the most ruthless types are raging in several areas of the world. The one in Algeria has become the most notorious. . . .

This grievous drama has continued for only too long. Should the two parties encounter difficulties regarding the modalities and guarantees of the application of self-determination, the United Nations should intervene immediately—through an impartial international commission—to organize, control, and supervise the referendum whereby the Algerian people shall freely determine the future of their entire country. This is a duty which the United Nations, true to its basic mission of safeguarding peace and protecting fundamental human rights, cannot lightly abdicate.

Another colonial war of equal ruthlessness and inhumanity is the one that is being waged against the defenseless people of Angola. . . . The United Nations cannot be expected to sit back as passive spectators to this frightful tragedy. A solution could and should be found—a solution based on right, on justice, on respect for the dignity of man and the right of the Angolan people to self-determination.

. . . I am also thinking of the Congo . . . Our policy has always been, and continues to be, the support of international efforts to preserve the sovereignty, unity, and territorial integrity of the young republic, to safeguard it from outside interference, and thus to insulate it from the arena of the Cold War. . . . The duty of the world community now is to continue to do everything in its power to erase the consequences of the sad experiences of the past. Foreign intervention, overt or covert, from which the Congolese people have suffered so grievously during the past year, should not be repeated. The Congo must be enabled to embark freely upon the road of its independent development based on respect for its sovereignty, unity, and territorial integrity. We should do this not for the sake of the Congo alone: if the Congo is allowed to drift into anarchy or civil war, or to fall, as a easy prey, into the clutches of foreign interference, the consequences of these things will not stop at the frontiers of the Congo. It will engulf the whole African continent. . . .

One of the poisonous phenomena from which mankind is suffering to-day is the practice of racial segregation and discrimination . . .

It is . . . our duty here to denounce the continuation of such policies and appeal to the conscience of man to take the necessary measures to discard this dangerous myth which is disturbing the happy relations between individuals and nations. In so doing we shall have achieved peaceful co-existence between the races, irrespective of their color or creed, on a basis of respect, equality, and dignity.

A constant source of anxiety and unrest in the Middle East for the last thirteen years has been the unsettled question of Palestine and the tragedy of the Palestinian Arab refugees. . . .

. . . we must state frankly that the United Nations bears a great responsibility for finding a just solution to this problem. We feel that a just and civilized solution is long overdue. But any solution which overlooks the facts and origins of the problem is bound to be a false one and cannot endure. The search for any such solution must start from the basic premise that the refugees will be given, in freedom, the right to determine their future by choosing either to return to their homes or to be fully compensated for their losses, as has been decided by the United Nations in about a dozen of its resolutions. The world cannot afford to allow this tragedy to continue and gain in magnitude and ramifications as time marches on. . . .

Yet another cause of the existing unrest and disharmony on the international scene can be found, in our view, in the disparity in the economic and social fields which characterizes our present time and divides the world into the very rich and the very poor. These unbalanced standards of economic development . . . sow the seeds of discontent and jealousy. . . .

The sharpness of this disparity has not been smoothed to an appreciable degree by the bilateral or multilateral assistance offered in the post-war era by some industrially developed countries, as these types of assistance were motivated in most cases by short-term political aims and were not based on genuine long-term economic and social policies. . . .

This type of conditional and meager assistance offered by the developed countries from the surplus of their accumulated wealth will not solve the problems of the underdeveloped countries. Accordingly, we believe we are justified in urging that all assistance to the poor countries should be channeled through the United Nations and its specialized agencies. At the same time, the developed countries should be urged to increase the amount of their assistance. And, in this respect, we believe that if we could come to an agreement on complete disarmament, there would be released huge funds which could be directed to enhancing the economic development of the poor countries and raising their standards of living. Moreover, the developed countries could prove their goodwill and cooperation by facilitating the task of the Commission on International Commodity Trade in exploring ways and means of stabilizing the prices of primary products, and, consequently, strengthening the economies of the underdeveloped countries by protecting them against fiscal fluctuations. . . .

Lastly, we are aware that the underdeveloped countries themselves should share in shouldering the responsibilities of putting an end to the economic and social differences prevailing in their countries and in different regions of the world. They must aim at economic as well as social development, thus avoiding the shortcomings of the Industrial Revolution. . . .

The United Nations may have made mistakes in the past. It may make more mistakes. But this is only natural. It is a human endeavor. . . .

What happened in the Congo is a most lucid example. It is an example of the kind of challenge that can face this Organization. It is an example, alas, of the way in which some Members can circumvent the decisions of the Organization. It is also an example of the extent of the sacrifices which some Member States can make to uphold the decisions of the Organization. . . .

Of course, there are weaknesses in the Organization. . . . One main weakness, for example, is caused by the exclusion from this community of the representatives of the People's Republic of China. . . . If this Organization is to be a true community of nations, it cannot close its doors to a quarter of the inhabitants of the globe. . . .

In order to strengthen the United Nations and enable it to meet many of the requirements of present-day international political life, we believe that the Charter of the United Nations should be amended. The world has changed since 1945. The membership of the Organization has doubled. Many young, energetic states have emerged, influencing by their vigor and youth the form and spirit of the Organization. Its activities, especially in the functional field, are expanding very fast. These drastic changes in the facts of international life make corresponding changes in the structure of the United Nations organs imperative.

I have in mind the expansion of the Security Council and the Economic and Social Council, so as to provide an adequate and just representation for all, especially the newly independent states from Africa and Asia. The use of the veto in the Security Council should, we believe, be curtailed, if not altogether abolished.

The United Nations Charter should also be amended to ban the production of nuclear weapons for military purposes and to condemn the armaments race. It should be amended to put an end to the myth of interference in the internal affairs of states, which crops up whenever the fate of a colonial people struggling for their liberation is brought to the attention of this Organization.

The main powers of the Organization should be concentrated in the General Assembly, as the most representative organ, and its decisions should have an effective mandatory character.

The scope and authority of the specialized agencies of the Organization should be expanded and strengthened in order to enable them to accentuate their most commendable efforts in the service of humanity.

About the current controversy regarding the office of the Secretary-General . . . We do not believe that the substitution of one Secretary-General by a triumvirate body with possible veto rights will in any way strengthen the executive arm of the Organization. . . .

Mongi Slim

Chairman of Tunisian Delegation to the UN
President of the Sixteenth Session of the General Assembly

. . . Today the Organization itself is being reappraised, not merely in regard to its geographical location, its administrative structure, and its methods, but also, and primarily, in regard to the fundamental meaning of its existence and of the permanent principles by which it is guided, as they derive from the Charter. Such a reappraisal has never before been made so insistently, so seriously, or so disquietingly. Until now, the United Nations has constituted the supranational framework within which conflicts of interest between nations could be at least attenuated, if not solved. Negotiations undertaken to that end have been based on the twin principles of tolerance and cooperation, which of necessity imply mutual understanding and reciprocal concessions in conformity, of course, with the requirements of law and justice. The Organization has been erected and maintained on the basis of the fundamental principle of equality among nations, whether great or small, strong or weak.

. . . the United Nations is suffering, today, from a moral crisis of humanity and its leaders . . .

This moral crisis . . . is, we feel, reflected in the desire recently shown by some to induce others to accept, and almost perforce to embrace, their opinions. The small countries of Africa and Asia are at times insistently urged to adopt one or another form of dogma. No sooner do we recover our freedom than we are invited to give it up, and let others interpret international problems for us and tell us what our position with regard to them should be. We have also been invited to consider ourselves a third, integral, African or African-Asian bloc, having as its sole catechism the breviary of statistics reflecting our regrettable state of underdevelopment.

The sacrifices which the people of Tunisia has had to make in order to

⁴ Fifteenth Session, *Official Records*, 897th Plenary Meeting, October 10, 1960.

recover the right to freedom of judgment and choice is still, in fact, too fresh in our memories for us to have any inclination to abandon that freedom in haste. Firmly attached to its policy of nonalignment, Tunisia cannot easily embrace a policy of general, systematic alignment. To us it seems more realistic, and more in accordance with the principle of free and peaceful coexistence between equal nations, to maintain our position of nonalignment, which enables us to bear our own responsibilities in regard to each problem on the basis of its merits and of the requirements of law and justice. What is more, we are convinced that it would not be in the interests of the United Nations, and would be still less in those of our African, the Asian, or even the American continent, for us to embark on such an adventure without weighing its implications very carefully.

The Tunisian delegation could not, in the name of what is commonly called political realism, agree to regard the division of the world into blocs of nations or coalitions of interests as something final. We do not wish to subscribe to the idea that peaceful coexistence is only a moment of respite vouchsafed to mankind. Such a prospect would mean not only a denial of the very principles of the Charter but indeed the end of coexistence among nations, and a sort of collective suicide by persuasion. . . .

The Tunisian delegation therefore opposes the division of the United Nations into three blocs, reduced to the status of offices or institutions. It is even more strongly opposed to the splitting of the United Nations executive into a sort of triumvirate.

The veto in the Security Council is even now distasteful to most Member States, because it runs counter to the principle of the equality of all states and gives to a few the power of thwarting the will of the majority. Its effects are counteracted to some extent by the Uniting for Peace Resolution [377(V)] which has already, four times, made it possible to call the General Assembly into emergency special session with a view to avoiding serious situations that might have gravely endangered international peace and security.

But the great majority of Members of our Organization continue to hope that this veto will be replaced by a more democratic system . . .

To transform now, or seek to transform, the office of Secretary-General into an organ which could also exert some sort of veto on the implementation of our Organization's decisions would undoubtedly result in rendering the United Nations ineffective. . . .

Small states like Tunisia are, first and foremost, interested in having a coherent, a strong, and, in particular, an effective international organization. The problems facing us in our efforts to speed up the independence of our brothers now fighting in Algeria, Africa, and elsewhere in the world, to consolidate our sovereignty and to rationalize our economic situation, all impose on us the duty of supporting the United Nations and the unity of its executive more than ever, and of urging authority and prestige for it, so that it may aid us more effectively in a struggle which is often one-sided and arduous. . . .

For us Tunisians—and we do not think we are alone in holding this view—the Algerian war is more than ever a test, which will enable us to estimate the real, practical value of the principles, and the moral capacity, of the Organization and its Members. . . .

Other states have not been vouchsafed the aid which, thanks to the United Nations and by its agency, the Congo has received in the organization of its administrative system. All this invests the Congo experiment with its significance and value on the plane of international relations. If this experiment were completely successful, it would constitute a promising precedent for the peaceful solution of decolonization problems. . . .

My delegation deeply regrets that the Cold War, the effects of which are so disastrous for international peace, has also become a factor exploiting the Congo situation for its own purposes.

The execution of the Security Council's decisions concerning military or civil assistance to the Congo has been the subject of criticism. My delegation still believes that the action taken by the United Nations in the Congo is in conformity with the Security Council decisions. In all honesty and objectivity, we can only pay a tribute to the Secretary-General, whom that body entrusted with the implementation of those decisions, and to his representatives, for the untiring devotion with which they have performed this really impartial task of peace and international solidarity. . . .

The experience in the Congo has for us a symbolic significance in that it has raised the problem of decolonization in one complete instance and in all its aspects—administrative, political, military, economic, and social. . . .

The delegations from Asia, Africa, and Latin America are perfectly familiar with the economic and social aspects of national emancipation and their importance in the process of decolonization. This awareness, among the communities of the third world, of the extent and gravity of their underdevelopment is a well-known sociological phenomenon. . . .

. . . if the underdeveloped countries are to develop reasonably quickly and as international stability and cooperation require, foreign aid in the shape of capital investment and personnel is essential. That aid is a duty insofar as it is agreed that underdevelopment is primarily the consequence of colonial expansion. It is also a measure of justice insofar as the exploitation of these countries' resources and the trade derived from such exploitation have been achieved at the expense of the communities ruled. Such aid, supplementing the efforts and sacrifices necessarily made by the newly independent peoples themselves, will give to the phenomenon of

decolonization its full meaning, by opening for our countries the way to a
rapid and harmonious restoration of their economic and social structures.

Kwame Nkrumah
President of the Republic of Ghana[5]

The great tide of history flows, and as it flows it carries to the shores of
reality the stubborn facts of life and men's relations one with another.
One cardinal fact of our time is the momentous impact of Africa's awaken-
ing upon the modern world. The flowing tide of African nationalism
sweeps everything before it and constitutes a challenge to the colonial
powers to make just restitution for the years of injustice and crime committed against our continent.

But Africa does not seek vengeance. It is against her very nature to har-
bor malice. Over 200 millions of our people cry out with one voice of
tremendous power—and what do we say? We do not ask for death for
our oppressors; we do not pronounce wishes of ill-fate for our slave-
masters; we make an assertion of a just and positive demand; our voice
booms across the oceans and mountains, over the hills and valleys, in the
desert places and through the vast expanse of mankind's habitation, and it
calls out for the freedom of Africa . . . It is a simple call, but it is also . . .
a red light of warning to those who would tend to ignore it. . . .

I look upon the United Nations as the only organization that holds out
any hope for the future of mankind. Cast your eyes across Africa: the
colonialists and imperialists are still there. In this twentieth century of
enlightenment, some nations still extol the vain glories of colonialism and
imperialism. As long as a single foot of African soil remains under foreign
domination, the world will know no peace. The United Nations must
therefore face its responsibilities, and ask those who would bury their heads
like the proverbial ostrich in their imperialist sands, to put their heads out
and look at the blazing African sun now traveling across the sky of Africa's
redemption. The United Nations must call upon all nations that have
colonies in Africa to grant complete independence to the territories still
under their control. In my view possession of colonies is now quite incompatible with membership in the United Nations. . . .

I would suggest that when the Charter of the United Nations comes to
be revised, a permanent seat for an African nation should be created on the
Security Council, in view not only of the growing number of African Members of the United Nations, but also of the increasing importance of the
African continent in world affairs. This suggestion applies equally to Asia
and to the Middle East. . . .

[5] Fifteenth Session, *Official Records*, 869th Plenary Meeting, September 23, 1960.

The Congo question is a test case for Africa. What is happening in the Congo today may happen in any other part of Africa tomorrow, and what the United Nations does today must set a precedent or a pattern for what it may have to do tomorrow. The United Nations will be judged by the success or failure of its handling of this Congo situation.

Certain propositions seem to me to be self-evident. The first of these is that the United Nations need not go to the assistance of any country which invites its intervention, but that once it has done so, it owes an obligation to the government and people of that country not to interfere in such a way as to prevent the legitimate government which invited it to enter the country from fulfilling its mandate. In other words, it is impossible for the United Nations at one and the same time to preserve law and order and to be neutral between the legal authorities and the law breakers. That is, unfortunately, exactly what the United Nations has attempted to do in the case of the Congo, and that is the cause of all the present difficulties and disagreements. . . .

I am sure that the independent African states will agree with me that the problem in the Congo is an acute African problem which can be solved by Africans only. I have on more than one occasion suggested that the United Nations should delegate its functions in the Congo to the independent African states, especially those African states whose contributions in men and materials make the United Nations effort in the Congo possible. The forces of these African states should be under a united African command responsible to the Security Council, in accordance with the first resolution of the Council under which the United Nations troops entered the Congo Republic [S/4387].

. . . The Congo, including Katanga and Kasai, is one and indivisible. Any other approach is mere wishful thinking, for not all the mineral wealth in that integral part of the Congo can create Katanga as a separate state.

The crisis in the Congo must be arrested now before it sparks off another world conflagration. . . .

It is quite clear that a desperate attempt is being made to create confusion in the Congo, extend the Cold War to Africa, and involve Africa in the suicidal quarrels of foreign powers. The United Nations must not allow this to happen. . . .

I would go further and suggest that all financial aid or technical assistance to the Republic of the Congo should be arranged only with the legitimate government of that republic channeled through the United Nations and guaranteed and supervised by a committee of the independent African states, appointed by the Security Council, which should be accountable to the United Nations. . . .

For thirteen years now the Union of South Africa has consistently disregarded the requests of the United Nations in regard to South West Africa. . . . It is the duty of the United Nations to enforce the mandate and the United Nations must not fail in this duty.

. . . The Union of South Africa should be asked to surrender the mandate to the United Nations and a committee of all the independent African states should be set up to administer the territory on behalf of the United Nations. If the Union of South Africa is unable to agree to this, then the next session of the General Assembly of the United Nations should take steps to terminate the mandate, make the territory a trust territory, and appoint the independent African states as administering authority.

I now turn to the Union of South Africa itself. The Union government, against all moral considerations and against every concept of human dignity, self respect, and decency, has established a policy of racial discrimination and persecution which in its essential inhumanity surpasses even the brutality of the Nazis against the Jews.

The interest of humanity compels every nation to take steps against such an inhuman policy and to act in concert to eliminate it from the world. . . .

The untenable claim of a minority in South Africa is steadily building a wall of intense hate which will result in the most violent and regrettable consequences in the future unless this minority abandons the iniquitous racial policy which it pursues. . . .

In Portuguese Africa there exists forced labor which is akin to slavery, all political freedom is denied, and, though it is difficult to believe, the condition of the ordinary African is worse even than it is in the Union of South Africa. . . .

In regard to Portugal, my view is that a particular responsibility rests on the NATO members who are also Members of the United Nations. They can bring pressure to bear on Portugal to accord the same independence to her colonies in Africa as other NATO powers have granted to their former colonial possessions. . . .

. . . it is essential that we on the African continent take positive steps to isolate ourselves as far as is possible from the effects of nuclear warfare. One of the first and most practical steps which could be taken in this regard is to prevent any state having nuclear weapons from possessing military bases on the African continent.

This is one of the main reasons why the government of Ghana believes that no African state should enter into an alliance of a military nature with any outside power. Any such alliance not only involves the state concerned in the risk of being drawn into nuclear warfare; it also endangers the security of the neighboring African states. . . .

I therefore make the positive proposal that whatever other steps may be taken to effect nuclear disarmament, a start should be made by all nuclear powers agreeing to keep Africa out of their nuclear warfare plans. . . .

And here I must refer in particular to the question of French atomic tests in the Sahara. The element of French intimidation contained in the tests was a positive provocation to Africa and a threat to world peace. We have no doubt that France chose the Sahara to demonstrate to African states their political weakness. . . .

In Africa we judge the Great Powers not by their words but by their deeds. We have a right to know which of the Great Powers support atomic tests on African soil, which of them oppose these tests, and, perhaps more important than everything else in assessing the situation, which of the Great Powers hold African opinion in· so little regard that, though in their hearts they oppose the French action, they are prepared to sacrifice African friendship in the interests of appeasing French pride and ambition. . . .

The responsibility for keeping the Cold War out of . . . Africa, rests . . . on the United Nations.

Louis Lansana Beavogui

Minister of Foreign Affairs of the Republic of Guinea[*]

To the manifold reasons for international tension, the death of Secretary-General Hammarskjöld is an additional factor which darkens a picture already too somber and ominous. The Afro-Asian group cannot remain indifferent to the tragic circumstances in which the sixteenth session of the Assembly opens. More than any other spiritual family or any other political group in the United Nations, the Afro-Asian group is in duty bound to voice its concern and its shock at the brutal disappearance of the chief executive of our Organization, . . .

For our delegation . . . there can be no doubt whatever that Secretary-General Hammarskjöld fell a victim of the same colonialist and racist forces whose united front, organized and financed in broad daylight, after having murdered Patrice Lumumba and his companions, is now endeavoring to prevent at any cost the inevitable decolonization of Central and Eastern Africa. . . .

This last crime, in any event, confirms our deep conviction that decolonization is the key problem which, more than any other, conditions the maintenance of international peace and security and the achievement of the major objectives of the United Nations Charter.

. . . it behooves us to proclaim at this rostrum the urgent need to extend the decolonization wherever that proves necessary, and, in particular . . . the vital need to bring the structure of the United Nations into line with

[*] Sixteenth Session, A/PV.1020, October 2, 1961.

contemporary realities . . . to give Africa and Asia the place which those two continents can legitimately claim in the principal organs and specialized agencies of our Organization. . . .

We remain virtually absent from the principal organs in which the decisions of our Organization are actually elaborated and effectively implemented. Even once admitted, Africans and Asians cannot escape the impression that they are not fully-fledged Members. They will not remain content with making statements. They wish to become associated with the principal organs and the specialized agencies, and thus to become a real part of the life of this United Nations. . . .

We are fully aware that . . . revision [of the Charter] calls for the agreement of the permanent members of the Security Council, but we must bluntly face those powers with their responsibilities in this very important field and invite them to reach speedily the minimum agreement necessary to bring about the changes which are so imperative. . . .

Our desire is that our Organization should promptly be provided with . . . an executive, who would be both effective and impartial. . . . Our choice should fall on a completely independent candidate who has integrity and competence. Such a candidate must of necessity come from a country which is independent, a country pursuing an effective nonalignment policy. In this regard we proclaim that we shall openly oppose and solemnly denounce any candidacy put forward in the context of the Cold War if it involves a candidate—even if it be an African or an Asian—who agrees to play the game of the blocs which are pitted against one another in this Organization. . . .

. . . we maintain it is vital that within the Security Council, the Economic and Social Council, and all principal organs of the United Nations, equitable representation be assured to Africa and Asia. This objective can be attained thanks to two procedures which we consider to be complementary: the redistribution of existing seats which can be undertaken whenever an election takes place, and an increase in the number of seats within these organs. This increase clearly would call for an amendment of the Charter under the conditions provided for in Article 108. This redistribution of seats and this increase in the number of seats seem essential to us; they are essential as a matter of justice and dignity. . . .

What we seek is an autonomous and genuine representation of Africa and Asia in the specialized agencies and in all United Nations organs, including the Secretariat. This objective can be obtained by simple amendments of the Charter just as the redistribution of existing seats can be obtained amicably by means of a change pursuant to new negotiations in the "Gentlemen's Agreement" which was concluded in London in 1946. But to enable Africa and Asia to make a full contribution to the life of the

United Nations, a fundamental amendment and revision of the Charter is necessary. . . .

. . . we should definitely rid our Organization of all the structures established in 1945 to deal with colonies and trust territories—structures which the colonial powers had succeeded in establishing and maintaining so as to drag the United Nations into their colonial ventures. More concretely and more specifically, the trusteeship system should be simply eliminated since it has proved that it was less favorable than the conventional system of individual colonization for the speedy emancipation of subject peoples. . . .

The total absence of Africa and the partial absence of Asia from the club of the Great Powers, permanent members of the Security Council, is another fiction which has lost any meaning. It is essential, if the veto is to be maintained, that Africa and Asia should be fully associated in this right so that they can bring their weight to bear in the settling of the broad international issues. . . .

San Francisco represented a glorious dawn for all the peoples who, at the end of the Second World War, had recovered or safeguarded their liberty. It is paradoxical and regrettable that at San Francisco the representatives of these very peoples did not definitely condemn colonialism. Thus, it would have been possible to unmask racial discrimination, obscurantism, underdevelopment, and the want and misery which enable the colonizers to live in peace, jealously protecting the tremendous wealth hidden in the sub-soil, waiting for the right moment to draw out the enormous profits, the moment when, as a result of extraordinary technological developments, the mining opportunities of old Europe will be diminished. . . .

Those are the evils of colonization which the worthy sons of Asia and Africa have denounced to the world, at the risk of falling prey to the insatiable wolves, the colonialists and imperialists. It is to put an end to these acts of the modern pirates that, in Algeria, Angola, the Congo, Rhodesia, Kenya, so-called Portuguese Guinea, and elsewhere, the blood of valiant patriots is still being shed; the supporters of war are using those countries as testing grounds for their arms and their technical developments. . . .

Our delegation deplores the fact that Portugal has deliberately and for a long time been guilty of a series of acts of indiscipline which are clearly incompatible with the obligations of all Member States. Thus my delegation is in complete agreement with the delegations which are asking that political, diplomatic, and economic sanctions should be taken against Portugal. . . .

To England, we say that it is not sufficient to publicize the history of decolonization to make us forget that our brothers from Bechuanaland, the Rhodesias, Nyasaland, Kenya, and other countries are still enslaved under the colonial yoke. What we expect from England is that it should immediately give freedom to the remnants of its colonial empire, because the peoples of these countries have as much right to that freedom as those that are already represented in our Organization.

To the Union of South Africa we merely say that it is in the interests of its European population to adopt a policy of nondiscrimination from the racial standpoint or it will have to bear all the responsibilities for the tragedy which the democratic revolution will visit upon its inhuman regime. The mandate of South West Africa, which has been acquired through the British Crown, must be revoked in order to allow the accession to independence of this martyred territory to take place. Until this is a fact we request that economic, political, and diplomatic sanctions be decreed against the so-called South African Republic and also against its accomplice Portugal which, since it has constantly challenged the conscience of humanity, must be brought back to reason in the interests of world peace. . . .

For the African delegations as for all other delegations which view as they should the fight for the national independence of the colonial peoples, the problems of imperialism and colonialism are directly linked with the problem of disarmament, that is to say, it is not possible to solve the one without solving the other. . . .

We cannot hide our deep disillusionment caused by the frenetic nuclear tests which have begun anew. . . . This gives us much cause for concern. That is why we condemn, categorically and without restriction, all nuclear tests. We address an urgent and solemn appeal to the governments of the Soviet Union, the United States of America, and France to take into account the concern felt by all people and to put an immediate end to all nuclear tests of whatever nature. We urge them to strive actively, in collaboration with the United Kingdom, for the conclusion of a final treaty prohibiting nuclear tests. . . .

. . . we denounce the trap that has been set up by the forces of domination and foreign economic and financial powers which want to maintain their domination in our country. . . . The numerous attempts made by the imperialist powers to establish economic communities and military alliances do not lead to a true solidarity among free and equal partners but only keep the poor in poverty and the slave enslaved. . . .

We want to use all the assistance offered to us on the one condition that our sovereignty and independence remain scrupulously respected. . . .

The direction of the affairs of Africa should be in the hands of the peoples of Africa, without any substitution of authority in political, economic, financial, military, social, or cultural matters. All that can be used politically in a positive manner in our fight for independence and the unity of the Africa peoples will constitute an important contribution to hastening the true emancipation of our peoples and the rapid progress of Africa, which is deeply desirous of being an instrument of international cooperation and an element of harmony and peace in the world.

It is in order to promote these efficient undertakings in the interests of the happiness of peoples and universal harmony that we have adhered to a policy of nonalignment. . . .

Our policy is not directed against any people, any regime, any country, or any man. The basis of our political action is not to destroy, but to build. . . .

Leopold Sedar Senghor
President of the Republic of Senegal[1]

. . . We have heard it said that the purpose of the United Nations is to maintain peace; others have said it is peaceful coexistence. But this is to confuse its aims with its purpose. Peace, as an absence of war, certainly is not sufficient in itself. We have also heard it said that the Organization was intended for international cooperation, because cooperation is based upon a positive element, a will for common union, a common vision of the future, a convergence of wisdom and of hearts—I might say, a coinspiration to speak . . . But why this common vision, this coinspiration, this coopera tion, if not for constructive purposes? But to construct what? Well, the international community—in other words, universal civilization which, rather than not existing, must be constructed of all our own original and particular civilizations. . . .

The first obstacle that we see when we consider the problems themselves is undoubtedly the Cold War, which continues between East and West, and which generates into a localized hot war sometimes. But you can be sure that this Cold War—which at times becomes a localized hot war—runs the risk of unleashing an atomic world war, from which there is no escape for all humanity. . . .

But the Cold War is an expression of only one of the fundamental evils; that which we must tackle are its roots. May I be permitted to remark that this evil derives from the imperialism of the great—to be exact—in Europe. . . . the roots lie in the spirit of dichotomy and Manicheism in Europe. . . .

If my analysis is correct, we have but one answer to give to the policy and spirit of imperialism, and that is to defend and maintain peace itself. Civilization is the expression of the community of man. Therefore, in order to create civilization, we must, first of all, live; and in order that men may live together, they must not hate one another; they must not wage war against one another. . . .

Talks as instruments of peace and international cooperation are the

[1] Sixteenth Session, A/PV.1045, October 31, 1961.

greatest contributions that can be given by the "third world," the uncommitted nations, and, particularly, by Africa. And Africa is more than ready
and willing to make this contribution to the United Nations. Why? Because dialogues—the famous African palaver, has been the essential element
of African tradition for thousands of years. It has been the political method
of Africa, because, without conversing and discussing, the thoughts and
reality of the antagonist being ignored appear to us as caricatures of themselves—because there is no absolute truth.

It is by the confrontation of opposing ideas that the true truth is born. . . .

In this struggle to wipe out the present forms of imperialism—whether
from the East or the West—the unaligned nations must courageously play
a major part. . . . We must affirm and assure that the principles of international morality will triumph, namely, freedom, equality, and fraternity
of races and nations . . .

However, the desire for truth compels me to confess that the great nations—Europe to which America will be added—are not only responsible
for the ills through which we are passing. Surely the moment has arrived
for us to carry out an agonizing reappraisal. There are too many nations
among the uncommitted, too many that at one time were colonized, and
that, unfortunately, caught the sickness of the one-time colonizers: the spirit
of intolerance and the hunger for conquest. You recognize imperialism
in any of its colors: brown, yellow, or black. Too often, those who vilify
colonialism loudest are those that claim the annexation of a sister state on
behalf of race, history, or even more unreasonable reasons, as though the
principle of self-determination were not valid and applicable to all peoples;
as though the nation necessarily coincided with the divisions of race or one-
time conquest or simply on the basis of appetite.

This Cold War, that we justifiably denounce, cannot be stopped except
by the "third world," by proclaiming our nonalignment, if we support
neither the East nor the West because they are our friends. As far as we of
Senegal are concerned, standing loyal to our friendship and to our commitments of cooperation, we wish to practice a consistent policy of nonalignment. We have given proof of this here in the Assembly. . . .

The [United Nations] Organization must be reorganized . . . The "third
world"—I mean primarily Asia and Africa—wants more seats in the
Security Council, claims more seats in the Economic and Social Council
and in the Secretariat itself; it seeks justice. This will, we submit, increase
the efficiency of the Organization to the extent that the "third world" is
determined to maintain its policy of nonalignment and negotiations. The
reorganization should not create insurmountable obstacles regarding the Security Council and the Economic and Social Council. However, the question of the veto in the Security Council cannot be side-stepped. It is true

that the two-thirds majority would be a better solution than the privilege or right of veto, but we must also be realistic.

. . . If the "third world" unites and perseveres, it can, in the long run, stop the use of the veto.

As far as the Secretary-General is concerned, to give it three heads is to institutionalize the veto at the executive level when it already exists at the level of decisions. The reasonable step to take would be to place next to the Secretary-General assistants chosen from the West, the East, and the nonaligned nations, to advise and help him. To personalize the question of the Secretariat would be to shut one's eyes and condemn the Organization to paralysis. I believe that the future Secretary-General should be neither from the East nor the West—I cannot say that he must not be white or a European, I merely say that he must be neither from the East nor the West. From what I have already said, and because you cannot be judge and party, he must not be uncommitted, he must not even be neutral, but he must be nonaligned. He must be someone whose culture and intelligence are at the level of his position. It would be wise for him to have, if not the agreement, at least the tolerance, both of the East and the West. . . .

But the basic problem still stands—the problem of disarmament. On its solution depends the solution of the Cold War, of which the Berlin crisis is only one aspect. On its solution, too, rests the maintenance of peace, without which, once again, there can be no international community nor can there be a universal civilization; there cannot even be a nation. . . . to disarm is to negotiate immediately to prohibit for all, everywhere and under all forms, any type of nuclear tests. Senegal has already condemned the French tests, even though they were limited in range and had only just started. Today we cannot but condemn the steps taken by the Soviet Union to resume nuclear tests.

. . . disarmament must stress the prohibition to manufacture thermonuclear weapons and bombs and the destruction of existing stockpiles; it must also bear on the control of disarmament, without which there could be no disarmament. This control must also be assured by the three parties: East, West, and the "third world."

I have already said that decolonization is intimately linked with the Cold War—the nameless war. The existence of colonies under any name, primarily in Africa and Asia, and the slowness of decolonization keeps the Cold War alive. Certain colonial powers are slow, mark time, try to maintain under new guises their one-time colonies, they try to replace their colonies by setting up a camouflage neocolonialism under the banner of ideology. . . .

As far as the United Nations is concerned all it has to do is implement the resolution voted on this question at the fifteenth regular session. This resolution was wise, it was also moderate, it did not set an imperative dead-line for independence and because it was wise and moderate it should be firmly and strictly applied. For reasons of justice and efficiency I think that we ought now to distinguish among the colonial powers those who de-colonize, despite everything, and those that stubbornly refuse to do so. Among the first we should place France and the United Kingdom; among the others we would put Portugal and South Africa, because internal coloni-alism is the worst of all. . . .

To refer now to France—in two years, from 1958 to 1960 it granted na-tional independence to fifteen dependent peoples, this is a fact. Some may challenge General de Gaulle's style, some may regret the mistakes made in his negotiations with the Maghreb, some might cast doubts on his sincerity, his will to achieve his end, but daily he risks his own life and that of his country. This is also one of the rare occurrences of the world. . . .

Regarding Portugal and regarding South Africa, I am surprised at the supine attitude taken by the United Nations and its weakness. I continue to believe that the Organization must be prudent in the use of military force, but I am astonished that the Security Council applies two standards, two weights, two measures, that it hesitates even to decide on economic and diplomatic measures to be taken against Portugal and South Africa, when it acts by force against Katanga. . . .

The rupture of diplomatic and economic relations with these two gov-ernments by the Members of the Organization is necessary because the honor of our Organization is at stake. Regarding Congo (Leopoldville) the attitude of Senegal has always been clear: we have always been in favor of territorial integrity and we have been against all secessions. . . . We do not oppose the decision of the Security Council which was to maintain the integrity of Congo (Leopoldville) if necessary by force. We only say that the representatives of the United Nations in Elizabethville lacked method and far-sightedness. If they had begun by expelling all the mercenaries and opposing the traffic in weapons Mr. Tshombé would have yielded without any military operation and Mr. Hammarskjöld would still be among us.

. . . Juridical independence without economic independence is a new type of dependence, it is worse than the first because it is less obvious. There-fore, the United Nations has a duty. If it wishes to obtain peace and achieve true decolonization it must organize economic assistance from the developed countries to the underdeveloped. . . .

There are 1,900 million inhabitants in the "third world," which has 17 percent of the resources of the world. The developed countries have 800 million inhabitants and they possess 83 percent of the world's resources. The gap is growing larger. The annual per capita income in the underdeveloped areas remains unchanged because in that area the 2.5 percent rise of the national income must cover a 2.5 percent increase in the population each year. In this "third world" the increase in the per capita income is much lower than it need be; $30,000 million of assistance should be extended to the underdeveloped areas whereas at present such assistance amounts to only $3,500 million.

. . . the difference between the two rates of growth has been systematically maintained by the developed countries through the device of trader economy. This policy consists of the artificial lowering of the prices of tropical raw materials and the artificial raising of the price of European manufactured products. . . .

. . . before the developed countries can assist this "third world" they must first of all re-establish the natural balance between the prices of raw materials and those of manufactured goods.

. . . Senegal believes that both [bilateral and multilateral] types of assistance should be maintained, with the understanding that multilateral assistance through the United Nations would be considerably increased on a percentage basis according to the national income of the developed countries. . . .

. . . we in the "third world" . . . are accustomed at times to speak harshly of the Great Powers I, also, have done this, but when all is said and done, are there no criticisms which we should make of ourselves? The truth is that by our ambitions, our weaknesses, and our errors, we have discouraged neither the arms race nor the Cold War. We have denounced the imperialism of the Great Powers perhaps in order to hide a lesser imperialism among ourselves in the "third world." We have sought disarmament on the part of the Great Powers while turning our own countries into arsenals. We proclaim neutralism but we do not always support this claim with a policy of true neutrality. It is time for us, the third or nonaligned world, to do our duty, if we truly wish to influence the Great Powers—and we should try in every way to do this. It is time to make our deeds match our words; it is time for us, in turn, to listen to the voice of reason and the voice of the heart.

Alhaji Sir Abubaker Tafawa Balewa
Prime Minister of the Federation of Nigeria[8]

Before proceeding to deal in detail with the many questions which are of interest to my country, it is better to state briefly the principles which we have accepted as the basis of our policies in international relations. First, it is the desire of Nigeria . . . to remain on friendly terms with all nations and to participate actively in the work of the United Nations Organization. Secondly, Nigeria, a large and a populous country of over 35 millions, has

[8] Fifteenth Session, *Official Records*, 893d Plenary Meeting, October 2, 1960.

absolutely no territorial or expansionist intentions. Thirdly, we shall not forget our old friends, and we are proud to have been accepted as a member of the British Commonwealth. But, nevertheless, we do not intend to ally ourselves as a matter of routine with any of the power blocs. We are committed to uphold the principles upon which the United Nations is founded. Fourthly, Nigeria hopes to work with other African states for the progress of Africa and to assist in bringing all African territories to a state of responsible independence.

It is perhaps natural that I should speak about Africa first. . . .

The recent tragic events in the Republic of the Congo must be uppermost in all our minds, . . .

. . . we in Nigeria feel there are several important factors to be constantly borne in mind in dealing with the problem.

The first of these is that Africa must not be allowed to become a battleground in the ideological struggle. For this reason the Congo situation must be a matter to be dealt with primarily by African states at the political level.

Secondly, we believe that in dealing with the problem of creating a real political life in the country itself it will be necessary to start at the bottom, by seeing that local and provincial authorities are established, while maintaining the essential unity of the country.

We also believe that the Congolese people were right to appeal to the United Nations Organization for help and advice in rebuilding their country, rather than to turn to any individual power. . . .

We warmly applauded the immediate response of the United Nations to the Congolese disaster. . . .

. . . there can be no question of the United Nations taking on the role of an administering power or of the Republic of the Congo being regarded as a United Nations trust territory. That republic has been declared independent, and if a practicable plan is to be worked out, we must accept the fact and arrange for assistance and advice, which the United Nations can give on an agency basis without infringing on the sovereignty of the government. . . .

Will the result be a confederacy or a federation? The root of the problem will lie in revenue allocation. And here the United Nations can be of the greatest assistance, by providing the necessary experts to inquire and advise. In all of its activities it is most essential that the United Nations make use of only the most able and experienced experts. . . .

We African states should come together to assist the Congolese to solve their problems. I feel sure that we can do so, but it must be done collectively and not done merely as so many individual states. We must do it together and we must be entrusted with this responsibility by the United Nations and be given its full backing. Nor would I limit advice and assistance to African countries, but would welcome the participation of other states, though, I repeat, I think it would be advisable to exclude the Great Powers.

Now to deal with the more general problems . . . The most serious problem in those cases seems to me to be that in itself political independence is totally inadequate if it is not accompanied by stability and economic security and if there is no genuine personal liberty, with freedom to express one's views and to profess whatever faith one desires.

. . . Spreading political propaganda or more insidious infiltration through technical assistance can virtually rob any underdeveloped country of its freedom. I therefore feel that if the advanced nations of the other continents are really desirous of seeing the new African states stand on their own feet and make their own particular contribution to the peace of the world and to the happiness of mankind, they should make a real effort to desist from fomenting trouble in any of the African countries. The best way for them to assist us in reaching maturity is not by spreading ideological propaganda, in whatever form it may be disguised, but by helping us genuinely, with really good will, to develop our resources and to educate our human material up to those standards which are necessary for proper development. . . .

The colonizing powers of the last century partitioned Africa in a haphazard and artificial manner and drew boundaries which cut right across former groupings. Yet, however artificial those boundaries were at first the countries they have created have come to regard themselves as units independent of one another. . . . It is . . . our policy to leave those boundaries as they are at present and to discourage any adjustment whatsoever. I hope that this policy will bring about an atmosphere of trust, and that if each country is given proper recognition and respect as a sovereign state it will be possible to have effective cooperation on all matters of common concern to us. . . .

We . . . believe in the United Nations as providing perhaps the only effective machinery for inducing world peace. But while proudly and gratefully accepting membership of this supreme world body, may I frankly say that we who waited for admission have sometimes been concerned lest our older and more powerful brethren are losing sight of the objective which, in founding this Organization, they sought to serve. If I think correctly, the whole purpose of this Organization is to enable the different countries to work together in a friendly atmosphere to procure the peace and progress of mankind, and this cooperation is meant to link all the Member nations, no matter what sort of government each individual country enjoys within its own boundaries. It was also, I believe, the intention of the original promoters to see that countries which are now backward should be assisted in every possible way to develop so that they become world assets and not liabilities. I do not think that it was ever the intention of any of those countries which were responsible for the creation of this Organization to turn it into an arena where party politics could be played on the highest level, and where ideological differences would obscure the main objective of securing peace among the nations and stability in the world at large.

. . . We are willing to learn before we rush into the field of international politics, but we are totally unwilling to be diverted from the ideals which we think true. That is the reason we in Nigeria will not be found to align ourselves as a matter of routine with any particular bloc. Indeed, I hate the very idea of blocs existing at all in the United Nations.

IN SEARCH OF A THREAD: THE UN IN THE CONGO LABYRINTH

Stanley Hoffmann

It is possible to distinguish roughly two periods in the history of the United Nations. During the first, which lasted until the middle nineteen fifties, the Western powers had a fairly secure majority in the General Assembly, and Cold War issues tended to dominate. The supreme test of that first phase was the Korean War. It showed both that the new International Organization refused to practice appeasement and that in a bipolar world whose main antagonists were engaged in an ideological struggle and endowed with nuclear weapons, UN intervention in the conflicts between the blocs would either expose the Organization to a demonstration of impotence or submit the world to the risks of escalation. A second phase began when membership of the UN increased, and the newly-independent nations became the biggest group within the Assembly. Now, as Dag Hammarskjöld put it in his report to the fifteenth General Assembly, the main task in the area of peace and security shifted to "preventive diplomacy"—rushing to the scene of fires which break out "outside the sphere of bloc differences" before the arrival of the major contenders. The biggest challenge has been the Congo crisis. It has tested all the assumptions which had been made—by scholars as well as by the late Secretary-General—about the role of the UN, its possibilities and its limits, and about the relations between its principal organs and its main groups of members.

It is as if a malevolent historical force had thrown into one pot all the separate problems with which the Organization had dealt, *seriatim,* in previous crises, plus some enormous new ones as well. It is as if the UN had had to play, at once, the role of three mythological figures. Sisyphus, of course, and, as usual, three times already the crisis appeared "almost" over, and the Secretary-General reported that the circle had been closed, only to discover that it was a vicious one. The Congo has also behaved as a Sphinx to the UN Oedipus: the questions which the Organization has been asked to answer have become increasingly tougher. Finally, the complications have been so great, and the moves of the World Organization have been so laborious, that one is tempted to compare it to Theseus looking for the Minotaur in the labyrinth; but Theseus, here, had no reliable thread.

STANLEY HOFFMANN is Associate Professor of Government at Harvard University and the editor of *Contemporary Theory in International Relations,* published by Prentiss-Hall, 1960.

It is impossible, obviously, to deal with all the facets of the crisis. I will limit myself to the period from July 1960 to January 1962, and I will not discuss either the financial aspects of the crisis, or the civilian operation in the Congo. I will concentrate on the attempts made by the political organs of the UN to find a thread, and on the lessons which can be drawn from the experience; but it is not possible to write a detailed history of those attempts in an article, or to arrive at peremptory conclusions at this stage. The reader will have to be satisfied with highlights, and with questions.

I. The Story

First phase: July 1960: In order not to lose our own way, we should keep in mind the distinction between the *end* of the UN mission in the Congo, and the *means* at the UN disposal. When the Congolese *force publique* revolted and Belgian troops intervened, a whole range of issues appeared: a) the problem to which two cables signed by President Kasavubu and Prime Minister Lumumba referred: the presence of Belgian troops; b) the breakdown of law and order, which had been the cause of their intervention; c) the danger of intervention from third powers as well, should the UN fail to cope adequately with the crisis. Already, on July 12, Vice-Premier Gizenga had appealed to the United States. On July 13, one of the cables mentioned threatened the UN with an appeal by the Congo to the Bandung powers. On July 14, Messrs. Kasavubu and Lumumba cabled Mr. Khrushchev;[1] d) the issue of the territorial integrity of the Congo—for on July 11 Mr. Tshombé had proclaimed the independence of Katanga.

The two cables of the Congolese leaders reqested UN aid exclusively on the first count—against what was termed Belgian aggression. The secession of Katanga was presented by them as an aspect of Belgium's conspiracy rather than as a separate issue. The "internal situation in Congo" was expressly ruled out from the request for aid.

Since the Republic of the Congo was not yet a member of the UN,[2] however, the Security Council met, not at the request of the Congolese leaders, but at the request of the Secretary-General, acting under Article 99 of the Charter. It is convenient, for the sake of analysis, to lump together the first two debates of the Security Council, the two statements made by Mr. Hammarskjöld on July 13 and 20, his first report of July 18, and the two resolutions of July 14 and 22.

As for the *nature* of the UN task, it became immediately clear that, con-

---

[1] For the text of those cables, see *Chronique de Politique Etrangère*, July–November 1960 (Vol. 13, Nos. 4–6), p. 668 and 696.

[2] Non-members can only appeal to the Security Council under Article 35, par. 2, i.e., in the framework of Chapter VI. See Michel Virally, "Les Nations Unies et l'affaire du Congo en 1960," *Annuaire français de Droit International*, VI, 1960, p. 557–559 and p. 563–564.

trary to the qualification given in the Congolese cables and to the terms of Soviet proposals, the UN action would not be an enforcement action under Articles 41 and 42, against an aggressor. It was not the Korean precedent that was being followed, but the precedents of all the other operations in which the UN had acted not as a soldier, but as a fireman. The precise legal basis of the UN intervention was not made clear (and remains in doubt), but the political nature was unmistakable.

As for the *objectives* of the UN, the situation was more complicated. One of the issues listed above was dealt with directly in both resolutions: the withdrawal of Belgian troops became the first objective. The restoration of law and order was the object of the key provision of the resolution of July 14—the one which authorized "the Secretary-General to take the necessary steps, in consultation with the Government of the Republic of the Congo, to provide the Government with such military assistance as may be necessary, until . . . the national security forces may be able, in the opinion of the Government, to meet fully their tasks." The goal of eliminating foreign interference was set in the second resolution; what foreign governments were asked not to do was "to impede the restoration of law and order and the exercise by the Government of the Congo of its authority"—not the only kind of interference, as one soon discovered. The issue of secession was alluded to obliquely—in the same sentence. Foreign governments were also asked to refrain from undermining the territorial integrity and the political independence of the Congo. Thus, for the time being the emphasis was being put only on the other three objectives, of which two were quite familiar. For the withdrawal of the invader and the insulation of the troubled area had been precisely the objectives of the UN in the crises of Suez and Lebanon.

As for the *means*, they consisted of the UN peace force created in accordance with the resolution of July 14. Here again, the thread suggested by Mr. Hammarskjöld was a familiar one; but here the trouble begins. On the one hand, the Secretary-General's statement of July 13 and report of July 18[3] defined the nature of the force as if the Congo were merely Suez and Lebanon revisited. Concerning the force's composition, troops from the permanent members of the Security Council would be ruled out. Concerning the mission of the force, it would "not be authorized to action beyond self-defence." It could not become a party to internal conflicts. It could not be used to enforce a solution of pending problems or to affect the outcome of political conflicts. On the other hand, however, the mission of the UN Operations in the Congo (ONUC) was not the same as that of the UN Emergency Force (UNEF) and the UN Observation Group in Lebanon (UNOGIL). In neither case had the UN been put in charge of

[3] S/PV.873, July 13/14, 1960, and Document S/4389.

assuring law and order within a nation. Mr. Hammarskjöld was applying to a particular set of objectives standards which had been effective in much narrower circumstances. Hence two problems arose, which were going to constitute the UN's main sources of trouble.

First, Mr. Hammarskjöld was raising a new issue—the role of the UN in the domestic disputes within the Congo. The settlement of those disputes was not to be a UN goal. It was indeed an issue which the two Congolese leaders had originally also ruled out of UN jurisdiction. But if those disputes were of no concern to the UN force, what was then the relation of the UN operation to the central government? During the months ahead, this would become one of the major bones of contention among the Members of the UN. Was the UN operation an arm of the central government? Did, on the contrary, the UN have the authority to tell the Congolese how they should govern themselves? The Secretary-General's very insistence on keeping the UN out of internal conflicts dictated his own answer, which was *no* to both questions. Secondly, by answering them in the negative, he was creating a crucial problem: the adequacy of the means to the end. Could a peace force whose activities were restricted by the principles derived from precedents really remedy the breakdown of law and order? The very terms of the agreement Mr. Hammarskjöld signed with the central government concerning ONUC showed that he realized that the precedents were not entirely valid. The Congo government stated that it would be guided by the fact that it had requested military assistance, and the UN affirmed that it intended to maintain its force "until such time as it deems the latter's task to have been fully accomplished."[4] If the restoration of law and order required a smaller degree of UN dependence on the consent of the host state (once consent to the creation of the force had been received), would it not require a revision of other principles as well—such as the defensive nature of the operation and its commitment to nonintervention?

Second phase: August 1960: The first test of Mr. Hammarskjöld's policy was the crisis over Katanga in August 1960. The doctrine which he developed in his report of August 6, in the addendum of August 12, and in his statements to the Security Council on August 8 and 21—and which the Council endorsed in the resolution of August 9—confirmed his original interpretation.[5]

The position of the Congolese government was simple. The objectives of the UN ought to be not only the withdrawal of the Belgians and the protection of lives and property, but also the maintenance of Congolese territorial integrity and the establishment of the central government's au-

---

[4] Addendum 5 to the Secretary-General's first report, Document S/4389.
[5] Document S/4417 and Add.6.

thority over all the country.[6] Those objectives could be met only if the UN force tried to reach them. What Mr. Lumumba was asking was that ONUC become the secular arm of his government, whose objectives would thus be recognized as those of the whole undertaking.

Mr. Hammarskjöld's interpretation was totally different. He continued to insist on a much narrower list of objectives. Relying heavily on the precedent of Lebanon, he distinguished between a) the UN duty to prevent outsiders from affecting political developments in the area (hence the need to get the Belgians out of Katanga) and b) the taking of a stand in internal political disputes. This amounted to saying that the two issues of political control in the Congo and of territorial integrity, both raised by political disputes among the Congolese, would not be among the concerns of the UN (except to the limited extent to which the resolution of July 22 had dealt with the latter). But if his interpretation of the objective was more restrictive than Mr. Lumumba's, his definition of the means rejected the Prime Minister's hierarchy. The UN force would not at all be at the disposal of the central government. It would enter Katanga to carry out the UN mandate, thus defined. But this definition also meant that the central government's authorities could not accompany or follow the UN forces, given Katanga's opposition to them. The combination of a mandate to preserve law and order throughout the Congo, and of a refusal to intervene in domestic disputes, insured that the "law and order" which would prevail in Katanga could only be that of the UN, but not that of the central government.[7] From the viewpoint of Mr. Lumumba, the UN was doing both too little and too much—too much, by reserving to itself a kind of monopoly of force; too little, by nevertheless refusing to use force itself and by sticking to a narrow definition of its objectives.

Mr. Hammarskjöld's conception was basically a prophylactic one: the role of the UN consists of extinguishing fires, of curtailing violence—both through insulation from outside interference and through elimination of civil war. But two fundamental questions can be raised about such an approach. First, does it not artificially separate the problem of the use of force (inside and outside) from the underlying substantive political issues? This distinction had already characterized the policy of the UN in the Middle East crisis of 1956.[8] There, UNEF intervened so as to get the British,

---

[6] See Mr. Lumumba's letter of August 14 in Document S/4417, Add.7.

[7] Addendum 6 to Document S/4417 states: a) that the UN force cannot be used on behalf of the central government to subdue the provincial government; b) that UN facilities cannot be used to transport civilian or military representatives under the authority of the central government to Katanga, beyond what follows from the general duty to maintain law and order; and c) that the UN has no right to refuse the central government to take any action of its own in accordance with the principles and purposes of the Charter.

[8] See the author's "Sisyphus and the Avalanche," *International Organization*, Summer 1957 (Vol. 11, No. 3), p. 446–469.

French, and Israelis out of Egypt, but the settlement of the disputes which had led to the explosion was kept quite separate from, and was pursued less vigorously than, the action of the UN to restore peace. Here, the UN, under the Secretary-General's guidance, was putting a ban on violence once again. But it was also passing a self-denying ordinance on the domestic political issues whose very existence was responsible for the resort to force. Those issues were supposed to be resolved peacefully by the Congolese themselves, and ONUC could not intervene except to preserve law and order. This was a police rather than a political conception of the UN role. But, precisely because the policeman was asked to shoot only in self-defense, the success of his mission depended on his not having too much policing to do— i.e. on a rapid settlement of those underlying issues in which he was not supposed to meddle.

Secondly, however, the somewhat artificial separation between the policing mission and the conciliatory function which had ultimately worked in the case of Suez, and which also succeeded in Lebanon because of a quick solution of Lebanon's domestic crisis, was much less tenable in the Congo. In Suez, a restoration of the *status juris* could stabilize, if shakily, the area for some years. In Lebanon, there was no general breakdown of law and order, and no secession. The trouble with Mr. Hammarskjöld's application of the precedents was that it not merely avoided the underlying political issues; it also made much more difficult the accomplishment of those tasks which he himself accepted. For, despite *and* because of his emphasis on nonintervention in domestic conflicts, he was undermining the central government. His reasoning on the nature of Katanga's secession is interesting. The problem, he said, stemmed neither from the presence of Belgian troops there, nor from "a wish of the authorities of the province to secede from the Republic of the Congo. The question is a constitutional one with strong undercurrents of individual and collective political aims."[9] Whether he intended to or not, the Secretary-General was thus questioning the political legitimacy of the *loi fondamentale* and the authority of the central government established in accordance with that law. The implications were not merely a return to the *status juris* of July 4, but a questioning of this status. Now, if the very constitutional foundations of the Congo were thus put in question, the consequences could not be other than disastrous. For, on the one hand, there was the risk of a vacuum of authority—the central government's being challenged by the definition Mr. Hammarskjöld had given of ONUC's task, but ONUC being, also by definition, prevented from substituting itself for the central government as the supreme political authority in the Congo. And on the other hand, the UN was not seeing to it that this vacuum be filled rapidly, since the ban Mr. Hammarskjöld was putting

[9] Document S/4417.

on the use of force by all parties to domestic disputes threatened to freeze chaos. As a result, the objectives of the UN—law and order, noninterference, and the departure of the Belgians—would be much more difficult to achieve. More violence and chaos were inevitable just as the Secretary-General was prematurely stating that the objectives had been reached. The next stage, he added, would be up to the Congolese people.[10] It was reconciliation and compromise he expected, but total bedlam he got.

Third phase: September 1961—January 1962: The events which followed the Security Council debate of August 21 are well known. Mr. Lumumba, who in July had threatened to turn to the Soviets for help if the Belgians did not leave within a few hours,[11] now asked for and received Soviet help in preparation for a drive against Katanga. His action led to his dismissal by President Kasavubu. The Premier in turn ousted the President. A new government, headed by Mr. Ileo, never became more than a shadow, since parliament never approved it, and since Colonel Mobutu seized what can hardly be called power. The phase which lasted from September 1960 to February 1961 was by far the saddest in the history of the Congo crisis—the winter of everyone's discontent.

On the one hand, the disappearance of any central government, the collapse of all institutions except a President with sharply curtailed powers under the *loi fondamentale,* and a parliament which was both deadlocked and dispersed, made of prophylaxy a pretty hopeless task. Belgian military and paramilitary elements and political and economic advisers were coming back both in Leopoldville and in Elisabethville. Foreign interference was inevitable. It was so obvious that the political vacuum had to be filled, that most of the interested states—i.e. practically everyone, big powers and Afro-Asian nations—took sides in the Congolese political battles. Finally, with the mushrooming of *de facto* authorities all over the Congo, arrests of political rivals, roaming private armies, etc., civil war on political as well as on tribal lines broke out repeatedly. Meanwhile, the two issues which the UN had not tackled directly before—the settlement of political differences and territorial integrity—also remained in suspension.

On the other hand, the United Nations did not revise its objectives and its means drastically. A few changes in the definition of the goals were made. Thus, in the first place, the General Assembly resolution of September 20 did, so to speak, make the connection between the prophylactic tasks and the domestic political situation. However, the barrage of nonintervention was not abandoned, and the Assembly, in conformity with a wish expressed in Mr. Hammarskjöld's fourth report to the Security Council,[12]

[10] S/PV.887, August 21, 1960.
[11] See Mr. Kanza's statement before the Security Council, S/PV.877, July 20/21, 1960.
[12] Document S/4482.

merely called on the Congolese for a speedy solution by peaceful means of all internal conflicts, with the assistance of African and Asian representatives appointed by the Advisory Committee the Secretary-General had set up. Thus the Assembly was taking cognizance of the issue which had become the crucial one—the issue of government. But the role of the UN remained limited to conciliation and good offices. The principle that the vacuum of authority had to be filled by the Congolese themselves still stood. Indeed, the same resolution repeated the words, now meaningless, of the resolution of July 14: the Secretary-General's task was "to assist the central government of the Congo in the restoration and the maintenance of law and order." In the second place, the goal of noninterference was faced more realistically. It had not been enough to ask states to refrain from undermining the central government. It was also necessary, in order for "preventive diplomacy" to succeed, to ask states not to lend arms or military personnel to any of the Congolese factions—not even to those which claimed to be the legitimate authority. Thirdly, the same resolution stated, less obliquely than in July, that the territorial integrity of the Congo was one of the objectives of the UN. But here again, implementation remained up in the air. The passage of the resolution to which I refer simply asked the Secretary-General to safeguard the Congo's unity.

A UN operation whose ends and means had been inadequate while there still existed a central government proved even more weak once disintegration spread. Two sets of difficulties became apparent in the new circumstances of quasi-anarchy. First, the distinction among *objectives* to which the Secretary-General was clinging became practically untenable. He still insisted on "the duty . . . to observe strict neutrality in the domestic conflicts."[13] As long as he had been able to give top priority to the task of external prophylaxy—getting the Belgians out and preventing other kinds of meddling—the main consequence of his insistence on nonintervention had been a conflict with the central government. The principal and immediate victim had indeed been that government. Now that it had collapsed, the most urgent problem was one of internal prophylaxy—avoiding all-out civil war. But with the performance of this task, the objective of nonintervention seemed incompatible. To insist on nonintervention endangered the UN operation itself. The reports of Mr. Dayal made it clear that the line to which his superior was clinging—that the UN force should do its best to preserve law and order, but should not intervene in domestic conflicts, even if it could be defended as an intellectual distinction or on purely legal grounds (as in the Secretary-General's statement to the Security Council on December 13)[14] —was of little operational value to the unfortunate UN authorities in the

[13] S/PV.896, September 9/10, 1960.
[14] S/PV.920, December 13/14, 1960.

field. The only way to avoid political intervention in a civil war is to stay out completely—and the precedent of the Lebanese constitutional crisis was simply irrelevant. Once one steps into such a situation, one intervenes whatever one does, or does not.

On the one hand *actions* undertaken by ONUC, and justified by the need to safeguard law and order,[15] could not but have a political result, even if they had no political intent. The decision of UN representatives to close the radio station and the airports of Leopoldville early in September, justified as a way of preventing a popular uprising, resulted in destroying Mr. Lumumba's hopes of regaining power. Later, the decision to prevent Colonel Mobutu's men from arresting Mr. Lumumba was justified by the need to avoid violence but denounced as political interference by Lumumba's enemies. As the harassed Special Representative noted in his second report, "almost every significant measure taken by ONUC, in the impartial fulfillment of its mandate, has been interpreted by one faction or another as being directed against itself."[16]

On the other hand, damned if it acted, ONUC was bound to be damned if it did not act—and one of the dangers of Mr. Hammarskjöld's fine distinction was that precisely since it did not indicate clearly what actions could be undertaken for the protection of lives and property without stepping over the line, it incited authorities in the field to *inaction*.[17] The consequences of inaction on behalf of political neutrality were catastrophic: political splintering and slaughtering. *De facto* authorities appeared in various parts of the country, and as Mr. Van Bilsen has remarked,[18] nonintervention indirectly consolidated all such changes even though they were brought about by force. Mr. Dayal and Mr. Hammarskjöld were reduced to severe criticisms of the irresponsibility and brutality of such local tyrannies. Mr. Dayal, instead of putting the blame on the principle he was trying to uphold, tended to use the Belgians as scapegoats in his reports.[19] As for violence resulting from UN inaction, the most spectacular example was the final arrest, deportation, and murder of Mr. Lumumba, whom the UN force considered to be beyond their protection once he escaped from Leopoldville.

[15] Or by the need to avoid foreign interference, such as Mr. Hammarskjöld's request to Belgium not to send any technical or financial aid to the Congo except through the UN (October 9 and 19; see Mr. Dayal's second report, Document S/4557).

[16] *Ibid.*

[17] On this point, see Robert West, "The UN and the Congo Financial Crisis," *International Organization,* Autumn 1961 (Vol. 15, No. 4), p. 603–617; and John Holmes, "The UN in the Congo," *International Affairs,* Winter 1960–61 (Vol. 16, No. 1), p. 1–15.

[18] A. A. J. Van Bilsen, "Some Aspects of the Congo Problem," *International Affairs,* January 1962 (Vol. 38, No. 1), p. 41–51.

[19] One should also mention the contradictions between cases of UN action, such as the closing of Leopoldville's airports, and instances of inaction, such as the fact that Elizabethville airport was left open when Lumumba landed there as a prisoner (cf. President Nkrumah's speech to the General Assembly, March 7, 1961).

As long as there was no central government with wide authority, law and order could not be preserved. The Secretary-General was quite right when he told the Security Council on December 7 that the creation of such a government had never been one of the objectives of the UN, that it was left to the Congolese and that chaos was their fault.[20] But the combination of a narrow UN mandate and of an unprepared, insufficient, and disintegrated Congolese political class was a vacuum filled only by violence.

Secondly, even if the limited objectives of the UN operation could have been kept apart from the political disputes which the UN wanted to avoid, the *means* at the disposal of ONUC were inadequate. On the one hand, the size of the peace force remained too small to contain civil war in a country as large as the Congo, and the Secretary-General was right again to remind those who wanted to increase the role of the UN in the Congo that they would also have to increase the means at the disposal of the UN. On the other hand, even a larger force would still have been handicapped by its status as a peace force. Mr. Dayal noted the heavy strain put on the soldiers by the duty not to use force unless in self-defense and "not to resort to military initiative in situations which would normally call for a strong reaction from courageous and responsible troops."[21] The essential task of insuring law and order could have been accomplished only if the UN forces had been able to disarm the multiple armies which were on a rampage throughout the Congo and whose actions Mr. Hammarskjöld himself had equated with genocide.[22] However, not only would such a forceful act have blurred the line between political intervention and the protection of lives and property, it would also have required a change in the nature of the force. To disarm only Mobutu's forces would have been a political choice. To disarm all of the Congo's bands would have been a giant undertaking.

The effect of those difficulties, which were the inevitable result of the UN mandate applied to conditions of civil war, was a double political crisis. In the Congo, the UN authorities ended by being on bad terms with every faction: not only with Mr. Lumumba's supporters, because of the events of August and early September, and later of the circumstances of his death, but also with President Kasavubu, the College of Commissioners and Colonel Mobutu, because of Mr. Dayal's sharp criticism of their behavior, and later of the UN failure to stop pro-Lumumba bands from seizing power in various parts of the country; and of course also with Mr. Tshombé, because of the UN insistence on a withdrawal of the Belgians. In New York, a major crisis developed between the Secretary-General and a large number of African and Asian nations, whose representatives, pointing out the perils I have

[20] S/PV.912, December 7, 1960.
[21] Document S/4531.
[22] S/PV.896, September 9/10, 1960.

tried to analyze, suggested a strengthening of the mandate. The UN operation was in an impasse, and there appeared to be two ways of breaking out of it.

If the UN stuck to its mandate, and the pattern of violence continued, the only way of avoiding the disintegration both of the chaos and of the UN operation would have been a withdrawal of ONUC—this was indeed the conclusion developed (no doubt in part for tactical reasons) by the Secretary-General before the General Assembly on December 19. If the UN could neither stand aside in the midst of civil war nor take sides—and since it was impossible for the force to interpose itself on behalf of law and order without appearing actually to choose sides—withdrawal could at least safeguard the future of the UN itself.[23] The other way of breaking the deadlock consisted, on the contrary, of realizing that ONUC would be condemned to a disastrous outcome as long as the UN did not, so to speak, wrest from the squabbling Congolese the initiative of trying to solve the domestic conflicts and restore a central government, as well as prevent the Congolese from aggravating those conflicts by the use of force on a massive scale. The choice was between getting out of the political vacuum which the UN had not received the mandate to fill, and having the UN fill the vacuum through a change of mandate.

The second solution would have meant a shift from Mr. Hammarskjöld's basic distinction and a strengthening of the UN means. But the discussions among the UN Members throughout the fall and the first half of the winter revealed that bold action by the UN could be as disruptive as the relative inaction for which Mr. Hammarskjöld was being blamed. There would be no peace in the Congo without a return to more "normal" political life. The Congolese seemed incapable of moving in such a direction. But the Members of the UN clashed violently about the direction which they wanted such a political life to take. In the discussions of those months, arguments about the UN mandate concealed intentions and interventions about the future of the Congo. To stay out of present Congolese politics was impossible. To get into the politics of Congo's future was divisive. Both "solutions" were explosive for the UN.

The evolution of what one might call Mr. Hammarskjöld's parliamentary situation is significant. So long as there had been a central government, the Secretary-General had received the firm backing of the Security Council, the Soviet Union's arguments and proposals had been rejected, and the Soviets did not use the veto. The first sign of a breakdown in the consensus was Guinea's sharp criticism of the Council's policy on August 21. But it was only when the central government collapsed that the cleavages among the Africans and Asians became clear. The Soviets seized the opportunity to

[23] A/PV.957, December 19, 1960.

widen the breach and to further polarize the situation by using their veto on September 17, thus transferring the problem to the General Assembly. Three months later, the previous consensus in the Council had disappeared,[24] and the consensus which had still been manifest in the special Assembly session on September 20 had also evaporated: the difference with Suez and Lebanon in the field was resulting in another and major political difference in the "parliamentary" situation in New York.

President Nkrumah, in the general debate of the regular Assembly session, had criticized the UN for having remained neutral between the law-breakers and the legal authorities.[25]   But the point was precisely that UN Members disagreed for political reasons as to who were the legal authorities. There were three possible but highly different handles with which the po-litical pot could be lifted from the Congo fire: the President of the Republic, Mr. Lumumba, and the Congo parliament (generally assumed to be favor-able, in its majority, to the deposed Premier).   To many nations of Asia and Africa, including some which had backed the Secretary-General's interpre-tation of the UN role (such as Ceylon and India), Mr. Lumumba repre-sented the legitimate political leader of the Congo, whether for political or for more legalistic reasons.[26]   The Western nations, however, chose to back Mr. Kasavubu, and the Assembly vote on the Credentials Committee's pro-posal to seat Mr. Kasavubu's representatives is an interesting one.[27]   From then on, the conflict opposed two factions.   On the one hand, there were those who, so as to bolster Mr. Kasavubu (who looked as if he needed time to win), argued for a restatement of the "Hammarskjöld line," and wanted it made clear that the initiative for a return to a normal political life would have to come from Mr. Kasavubu—meanwhile the UN mission would re-main essentially the defense of law and order.   Those nations' views about *who* should fill the political vacuum in the Congo coincided with Mr. Hammarskjöld's view about *how* it should be filled.   They hoped to reach their objectives through his procedure.   On the other side stood those who realized that a blunt proposal to liberate Lumumba and to disarm Mobutu's forces (as pressed by the Soviets) had no chance of being adopted; they sug-gested more moderately, but unmistakably in the same direction, that all political prisoners be released, parliament be reconvened, and measures be

[24] On December 13, Ceylon and Tunisia gave up the idea of submitting a draft; the four-power draft (Argentina, Italy, United Kingdom, United States) would have been accepted except for a Soviet veto, but Tunisia abstained and Ceylon joined the Soviet Union and Poland in opposing it.

[25] See *UN Review,* November 1960 (Vol. 7, No. 5), p. 33–35.

[26] On October 28, Ceylon, Ghana, Guinea, India, Indonesia, Mali, Morocco, and the UAR sponsored a draft resolution for the immediate seating of Mr. Lumumba's representatives (Document A/L.319/-Rev.2).

[27] The Assembly voted 53-24-19 in favor of seating Mr. Kasavubu.   But among the 53 states there was only one of the members of the Conciliation Committee (Senegal); seven members were among the opponents (Ghana, Guinea, India, Indonesia, Mali, Morocco, the UAR); and six abstained (Ethi-opia, Malaya, Libya, Pakistan, Sudan, Tunisia).

taken to prevent armed units from interfering in political life. When the matter came to a head before the General Assembly on December 19–20, Mr. Hammarskjöld, who had quite lucidly analyzed before the Security Council a few days earlier the disadvantages of a narrow mandate, did not speak out for a broader one. Both draft resolutions failed to be adopted. As a consequence, the UN remained tied by the previous resolutions and interpretations, which had exposed its weakness. The vicious circle was made more cruel by a series of troop withdrawals decided on by the states most hostile to Mr. Kasavubu, and more evident by the gap among African and Asian states which the rival conferences of Brazzaville and Casablanca exposed.

Fourth phase: February–August 1961: The first major change in the mandate of the UN was made by the Security Council in February 1961 (and confirmed by the General Assembly in April). The circumstances that led to it are highly significant. By the end of January, the situation of ONUC appeared pretty close to that brink of withdrawal about which the Secretary-General had been warning: Mr. Kasavubu was requesting Mr. Dayal's dismissal and summoning ONUC to help him subdue the pro-Lumumba forces in Stanleyville and Bukavu or threatening otherwise to seek help elsewhere.[28] The nations devoted to Mr. Lumumba were upset by his transfer to Katanga. Mr. Hammarskjöld's reaction was not to suggest that ONUC get out, but to advocate a stronger mandate. However even now it was only obliquely, or so to speak crabwise, that he was moving to let the UN deal with the political conflicts in the Congo. His approach remained a policing one. Thus, without advocating that the somewhat intangible barrier between "law and order" and political intervention be destroyed,[29] he preferred to operate through a change of his previous interpretation of the mandate to insure law and order. This objective, he now stated, did require a reorganization of the Congolese army which would take it out of politics. This was less than the "interposition" which he had rejected in December but more than the previous piecemeal protection of lives and property which left Congolese armed bands intact. It meant no break from his previously stated determination to limit the duty of the UN to

> unburden the authorities of the immediate responsibility for the protection of life and security and to eliminate foreign military intervention so as . . . to create a framework within which the people of the Congo could find its way to a stable government, enjoying adequate nationwide authority.[30]

---

[28] Document S/4643.
[29] However (see Document S/4606), the Secretary-General had informed Mr. Kasavubu of the strong conviction of almost all the Members that parliament should be convened.
[30] See note 14.

It simply equated such protection with the elimination of domestic military intervention as well. Nor did he propose a major change in the means of ONUC. He suggested that the army's reorganization (which, not being a disarmament would presumably not require the use of force) be done with the cooperation of the leaders concerned. Whether the scheme would have worked is hard to say.

Precisely, however, because this suggestion still seemed to respect artificial distinctions, those states which wanted the UN to fill the political vacuum in the only way which they accepted came forth with proposals for urgent measures to free Mr. Lumumba, reconvene parliament, and disarm Colonel Mobutu's forces. Once again, a deadlock seemed in the making, for the same reasons as in December. But one event drastically altered the picture: Lumumba's assassination. From now on, those who had been his champions had to choose between two alternatives. They could adopt the policy of vengeance advocated by the Soviet Union, which in a series of not very consistent proposals advocated on the one hand that the UN operation become a collective security enterprise, under Article 41, against Belgium, Mobutu, and Tshombé, and on the other hand that the operation be discontinued within a month. Or else they could keep pushing in the same direction as before—the return of parliament, the neutralization of Mobutu —even though the political results might well not be the same any longer. But from now on, those who had been most reluctant to move in such a direction because they felt that Lumumba would be the only beneficiary of these measures were far less unwilling to strengthen the UN mandate, as long at least as the objectives and means were not biased in favor of the murdered leader's partisans. Thus a rapprochement took place between the more moderate elements of the two camps into which the UN had been divided: the resolution of February 21, which had a close resemblance to the eight-power draft rejected by the General Assembly and opposed by the United States in December, was adopted in a vote in which the United States sided with Ceylon and the UAR; only the Soviet Union and France abstained. The seventeen-power draft endorsed on April 15 by the General Assembly, which incorporated the suggestions of the Conciliation Commission, and which did not differ much from the eight-power draft of December, received the support of three Asian states which had voted against the eight-power text, and of thirteen African and Asian states which had abstained previously. Of the seventeen African and Asian nations which had voted for the eight-power draft in December, six endorsed the new text in April, eleven abstained. Those shifts give evidence both of a rapprochement and of the traces left by past battles.[31] Indeed, those states which had

---

[31] The seventeen-power draft was endorsed by the Philippines, Thailand, and Japan which had voted against the eight-power draft on December 20; Cyprus, Burma, Lebanon, Jordan, Nepal, Paki-

most vigorously backed Mr. Lumumba tried, both in the Council and in the Assembly, to strengthen the mandate of the UN operation even beyond what the new consensus was willing to accept, and in such a way that the pro-Lumumba forces would gain from the UN intervention, but those attempts failed.[32] It is significant that the only states that voted against the seventeen-power draft on April 15 were, on the one hand, the Soviet bloc, and on the other, seven of France's former African colonies.

The resolution of February 21, 1961, and the two resolutions of April 15 defined the new UN mandate in the following fashion. First, as to the *objectives,* the issue which was, in a way, the oldest of all, Belgian withdrawal, was dealt with vigorously both by the Council and by the Assembly. Not only troops, but paramilitary personnel, political advisers, and mercenaries, were asked to withdraw. Noninterference by other states was also requested again, in sharp terms. The extension of the "law and order" mission of the UN to cover a reorganization of the Congo army, which Mr. Hammarskjöld had suggested, was endorsed by the Security Council. The touchy issue of domestic Congo politics was finally tackled by the UN. This time, the Council urged that parliament be convened, and the Assembly also asked for the immediate release of all parliamentarians. Secondly, as for the *means,* ONUC was empowered by the Security Council resolution to use force, if necessary, in the last resort in order to prevent civil war. The Secretary-General stated that the February resolution gave the UN a clearer and stronger framework but did not provide a new legal basis or new means of implementation. What he meant, one can assume, is that if there was a shift there was no mutation. On the one hand, UN meddling in Congolese political disputes remained limited to the suggestion of a procedure (the summoning of parliament). Thus the Secretary-General's distinction between law and order and UN responsibility for political settlement was theoretically still standing.[33] On the other hand, the transformation of the peace force into a shooting force was doubly limited, not only by the condition of "last resort," but also to the accomplishment of only one part of *one* of the objectives: the "law and order" goal, insofar as the prevention of civil war (not the new task of reorganizing the army) was concerned.

If the Secretary-General was more willing to stress the continuity of UN

---

stan, Iran, Malaya, Senegal, Somalia, Chad, Tunisia, and Liberia abstained in December, but voted for the draft in April; Ethiopia, Nigeria, Togo, Libya, Saudi Arabia, and Sudan voted for both texts; Ceylon, India, Indonesia, Iraq, the UAR, Ghana, Guinea, Morocco, Mali, Afghanistan, Yemen voted for the eight-power draft in December and abstained in April. The ex-Belgian Congo had voted against the eight-power draft in December and abstained in April.

[32] Draft by Ceylon, Liberia, and the UAR, Security Council, February 21 (Document S/4733); it dealt exclusively with incidents in Leopoldville, Katanga, and Kasai.

[33] Before Lumumba's death, the reconvening of parliament, supposed to be favorable to him, was a substantive move; now it became merely a procedure.

action, Mr. Kasavubu was more struck by the shift. Not only was he being told how to restore political life, but he was also being asked to discipline and reorganize his army—and in this repect the line of separation between the UN task of preserving order and the UN refusal to intervene substantively in domestic affairs was really invisible to the naked eye. Not too surprisingly, the Congolese President reacted at first by trying to solve the political crisis in his own way (Tananarive Conference) and Mobutu's troops reacted by attacking ONUC. But at Tananarive Tshombé, not Kasavubu, won, and gradually the Congo President came to realize that he had more to gain by working with the UN than by opposing it, especially since many of its members were still willing to strengthen the mandate so as to favor the Lumumbist elements in the Congo. Reconciliation was made easier by Mr. Dayal's departure from the Congo in March, followed by his formal resignation on May 26. On May 17, Mr. Hammarskjöld and President Kasavubu signed an agreement which substituted cooperation for conflict. With the assistance of the Secretary-General's new representatives, the main Congo factions came to an understanding about a new session of parliament. After the tragi-comedy of his arrest at Coquilhatville, Mr. Tshombé appeared to be willing to join the proceedings, and early in August, a new Premier, Mr. Adoula, reported to Mr. Hammarskjöld that the constitutional crisis of the Congo was over. The Secretary-General replied that he agreed to deal exclusively with Mr. Adoula's government. The UN appeared, for the second time, to have closed the circle. There was a central government in which Mr. Gizenga, the heir of Lumumba, participated. The talks about the withdrawal of Belgian elements were going well (especially since there was a new Belgian government also). Law and order appeared assured. There remained only the issue which trouble at the center had overshadowed for almost a year: Katanga.

Fifth Phase: September 1961–? At the center, it was to the extent to which a temporary settlement of political conflicts had been negotiated that it became possible *both* to reduce the amount of violence committed by Congolese bands and factions and to avoid a UN resort to force in implementation of the February resolution. But the absence of any political settlement between Messrs. Kasavubu and Adoula on the one hand, and the Katanga authorities on the other, endangered everything that had been achieved. It seemed to make a solution by force inevitable, with all its consequences for law and order, and it also threatened to destroy the political compromise of Leopoldville, by providing Mr. Gizenga with a powerful nationalist weapon. Just as inevitably, the UN authorities in the Congo were being pushed into a corner. If they did nothing, their Herculean work of the past would perhaps be destroyed. Should they not use force first, before the Congolese were at it again?

Once more, the alternatives seemed to be either impotence or an enlargement of the mandate. For the UN mission had been neither broadened nor strengthened with respect to Katanga. As for the objective of territorial integrity, as we have seen, it had been approached rather obliquely by the various resolutions. The best lever at the disposal of the UN was the presence of Belgian and other foreign soldiers and advisers in Katanga. The way to the objective of territorial integrity seemed to pass through "objective no. 1," although the Secretary-General had warned a year before that Katanga's dissidence was not merely a Belgian design. However, even that lever was not easy to manipulate, since the UN had not been allowed to use force in order to get to "objective no. 1."

The UN moves against Katanga came in three phases. The first was that of August 28, when UN forces in Elizabethville proceeded to arrest more than 200 mercenaries. The legal basis of the UN action, in this writer's opinion, is exceedingly shaky. The officer-in-charge, Mr. Linner, noted that the UN had previously lacked authority to act, but that such authority was provided by a request from the Congo government for assistance in the execution of a decree passed by the government for the expulsion of non-Congolese men serving in the forces of Katanga.[34] It is true that under past resolutions of the Security Council, the UN was supposed to assist the central government in the restoration of law and order. But ONUC had been authorized to use force only to avert civil war. What prevented a major political explosion at the time was the fact that the UN, which acted by surprise, met with no resistance, and that Mr. Tshombé endorsed the move.

A second one came two weeks later, and this time a battle broke out: this was the series of events which led to Mr. Hammarskjöld's death. The report of Mr. Linner is extremely discreet about the basis and circumstances. The UN representative in Elizabethville, Mr. O'Brien, has been less discreet.[35] Whether his version is entirely correct—as in any battle, each combatant is likely to take what he saw for the whole thing—I cannot say; but it is an intriguing one. According to Mr. Linner, the UN forces, which found themselves in a most dangerous situation, in the midst of sporadic attacks and an ocean of hostile rumors, had to resort to "security precautions similar to those of Aug. 28." This implied that the UN was acting both in self-defense and on behalf of the central government—a point which raised the whole issue of the relations between the government and ONUC, i.e., reopened the whole question of intervention in domestic affairs. Mr. O'Brien's account is less defensive; according to him, he had suggested that the use of force be based on the resolution of February 21 which authorized it to prevent civil war—but also that it be continued "until the secession of Katanga

[34] Document S/4940.
[35] See his two articles in the *Observer*, December 10 and 17, 1961.

. . . had been ended." Mr. Khiari, the head of UN civilian operations, arrived in Elizabethville on September 10 and instructed the UN authorities in Katanga to proceed as Mr. O'Brien had indicated: not only were the mercenaries to be expelled, but three of Katanga's ministers were to be arrested under warrants signed by the central government; "Mr. Tshombé also was to be arrested if absolutely necessary." If this version is correct, then a) it implies that there now existed between the central government and ONUC the very relationship which Mr. Hammarskjöld, precisely because of his emphasis on nonintervention in domestic conflicts, had constantly rejected;[36] b) it suggests what the French call a *détournement de pouvoir:* the use of a power conferred with respect to one objective, so as to reach another goal for which no such power has been granted; c) it reveals that the chain of command was quite extraordinarily lax; not only does Mr. O'Brien suspect that the Secretary-General never knew of Mr. Khiari's instructions, but Mr. O'Brien writes "it seemed entirely natural to accept verbal instructions from him (Mr. Khiari) in so important and secret a matter"! Mr. Hammarskjöld's reaction, reported by Mr. O'Brien as indicated by Lord Landsdowne who saw him in Leopoldville on September 16, and demonstrated by his message to Mr. Tshombé—in which he a) repeated that conflicts had to be settled by negotiation, conciliation, and mediation, and b) stressed the need for a cease-fire—can hardly be called endorsement of his subordinate's action.

But this action, in a way, was an anticipation of and an advance on the new mandate which marked the beginning of the third phase, in the Security Council resolution of November 24, 1961. The importance of the shift can hardly be exaggerated: the UN was doing now, under acting Secretary-General U Thant's leadership, what it had refused to do during the first Katanga crisis, in August 1960, under Mr. Hammarskjöld. The events which prompted the change were: the failure of Katangese authorities to carry out the February resolution concerning the mercenaries; the failure of efforts at reconciliation between Tshombé and the central government; the beginning of a new breakdown of law and order as a consequence of military operations by Generals Mobutu and Lundula against Katanga; and the fear of a collapse of the central government because of the failure to put an end to Katanga's secessions, in particular because of Mr. Gizenga's own behavior in Stanleyville. Fifteen months earlier, Mr. Hammarskjöld's use of preventive diplomacy had led both to more violence and to political chaos. This time, the UN redefined its mission in such a way that preventive diplomacy included both what can be called a preventive use of force and a clear-cut intervention in domestic disputes. It is ironical that the late Secretary-

---

[36] Lord Landsdowne reported that Mr. Hammarskjöld denied that the operation had been undertaken on behalf of the central government (*Observer*, December 10, 1961).

General's thread should have been discarded so shortly after, in the introduction to his last annual report, he warned the Members of the UN that whatever mistakes had been made,

> it is to be hoped that they do not lead members to revise the basic rules which guide the UN activities in such situations, as laid down in the first report of the Secretary-General to the Security Council on the Congo question, which the Council, a year ago, found reason unanimously to commend.[37]

The resolution of November 24 repudiated Mr. Hammarskjöld's doctrine on two points. Concerning the *means,* the acting Secretary-General was now authorized to use force, not only as a last resort against civil war, but also for the apprehension of all foreign military and paramilitary personnel and political advisers. But it is about the *objectives* that the biggest change took place: the principle of nonintervention in domestic disputes was now dropped, precisely because it seemed to stand in the way, not only of the mission to insure law and order—always in question as long as the political disputes persisted—but also of the goal of territorial integrity, which the resolution squarely endorsed by condemning all secessionist activities. On the contrary, so as to preserve law and order as well as to eliminate secession, the Council "declared full and firm support for the Central Government of the Congo" and urged all Members to support it. Whereas Mr. Hammarskjöld's stand on domestic conflicts had led him, on the one hand, to analyze Katanga's position not essentially as either a Belgian maneuver or a desire for secession, but as a constitutional disagreement which was beyond UN jurisdiction, the new analysis backed the central government's stand on the *loi fondamentale* and treated Katanga's position as merely an obstacle to Belgian withdrawal and Congolese territorial integrity. Whereas Mr. Hammarskjöld's stand on domestic conflicts had led him to adopt toward the central government of Mr. Lumumba an attitude of reserve, even, at times, reproach and certainly noncooperation as to the suppression of Katanga, acting Secretary-General U Thant urged "a sympathetic attitude on the part of ONUC toward the efforts of the Government to suppress all armed activities against the central government and secessionist activities."[38]

The *combination* of the means now at the disposal of the UN and of the new objectives produced in turn a third and very important change. Under Mr. Hammarskjöld, the two limitations of the restriction of the objective of law and order by the principle of nonintervention and the restriction of the right to use force to the goal of preventing civil war had reduced the resort to force by ONUC to a very narrow range of possibilities. This was no longer the case. The Security Council resolution of November 24 restated

---

[37] See *International Organization,* Autumn 1961 (Vol. 15, No. 4), p. 562.
[38] S/PV.982, November 24, 1961.

that ONUC was to assist the central government in maintaining law and order, but now that the principle of nonintervention was dropped, this restatement meant a mutation. In accordance with Mr. O'Brien's anticipation, it meant that ONUC in the future could use force to assist the central government if the latter requested such aid so as to preserve law and order—an indirect, but considerable, revision of the mandate, as it actually added a whole new range of possibilities for the use of force.

Since the passage of the resolution the UN has used force twice. The most spectacular instance, of course, was the "second battle of Katanga," which raged for more than ten days in December 1961 and the political reverberations of which are well known. Both the officer-in-charge and the acting Secretary-General have presented the UN operation as one of self defense, both to restore law and order in Elizabethville and to regain liberty of movement.[39] As an indication of the change of policy since September, this time there was no negotiated cease-fire agreement. Less noticed, but in some ways even more interesting, has been U Thant's decision to let ONUC assist General Lundula's efforts in Stanleyville to disarm Gizenga's *gendarmerie*. U Thant accepted "within the framework of ONUC's mandate to assist the central government in the maintenance of law and order and in the prevention of civil war."[40] What made of this decision a peculiarly remarkable move was the fact that it was taken even though the Soviets on November 24 had vetoed an American amendment aimed at condemning secessionist activities other than Tshombé's, i.e., Gizenga's.

As a consequence, Mr. Gizenga's demise has consolidated the central government, and Mr. Tshombé's military defeat has led to the Kitona agreement with Mr. Adoula. However, events of recent weeks have shown that Katanga's secession continues. Against Mr. Tshombé, the UN has barely begun to use its new mandate. It could resort to force again—either so as to expel those hydra-like mercenaries; or as an adjunct of the central government, should the latter ask the UN to assist it in restoring law and order in Katanga; or under an equally broad interpretation of its right to use force so as to prevent civil war. With the principle of nonintervention gone, such an objective as the maintenance of law and order (of which the avoidance of civil war is one facet) can be given a very, let us say, flexible interpretation. Nor is there any doubt that Katanga's continuing secession imperils all the present objectives of the UN—Belgian withdrawal, foreign noninterference, the maintenance of public order, a stable central government, and the Congo's territorial integrity.

[39] See *UN Review,* January 1962 (Vol. 9, No. 1), p. 6–7 and 44ff.
[40] See *ibid.,* February 1962 (Vol. 9, No. 2), p. 27.

II. The Lessons

The role of the UN: At this stage, a balance sheet of the UN operation in the Congo must begin by "accentuating the positive." Even if we leave aside the achievements in the field of technical assistance, we must list the following among the successes of the UN: a) Considerable accomplishments have been made in the mission of "external prophylaxy." Even in Katanga, the presence of Belgian military and political defenders of Mr. Tshombé seems now limited to men whom their government condemns and who stay in Katanga as Tshombé's pretorians, not as Belgium's rearguard. The intervention of other nations has been either channeled through the UN (US help to ONUC in Katanga) or limited to political pressure. b) Remarkable progress has been made in the solution of domestic problems: a large measure of law and order has been restored and a central government with wide authority has finally been established. Only Katanga's secession remains a major issue.

However, the undertaking has been a painful one, and the main lesson about the role of the UN may well be the following. On the one hand, just as events of recent years, including the Congo operation, have vindicated to a large extent the "Founding Fathers'" idea that the UN could not be effective unless there existed a concert of the big powers, the Congo crisis has shown that they were wise in assuming that the Organization's efficiency would also be imperiled if it intervened in the domestic affairs of states. On the other hand, the very nature of international politics condemns the UN to a choice between abdication, if it takes literally the warnings of the Charter, and turmoil accompanied by numerous remonstrations of embarrassment or impotence, if it disregards those caveats.

Mr. Hammarskjöld's policy was an attempt to find a middle way. There is a fascinating contrast between the fashion in which he used his own powers and the manner in which he interpreted the UN mission. Mr. Hammarskjöld was determined to have the Secretary-General play as large a role as conceivable. He used for the first time the power of initiative of Article 99. Secondly, as a result of the suggestions which he himself made to the Security Council and which the early resolutions embodied, he was given important mandates: to report on the military assistance provided by the UN, to act so as to obtain the Belgians' withdrawal, and (through the General Assembly resolution adopted in September 1960) to safeguard the unity of the Congo. Thirdly, he used with considerable imagination the power to interpret ambiguous resolutions and the power to carry out mandates, even though the political organs, paralyzed by dissension, failed to provide him with guidance. In this area, as he explained in his Oxford speech of 1961,[41] he was determined to act until and unless disavowed by the

---

[41] "The International Civil Servant in Law and in Fact," SG/1035, May 29, 1961.

political organs—and he was challenged at times, but never disavowed by any majority.[42]

However, where the role of the Organization itself was concerned, we have seen how subtly narrow the Secretary-General's concepts and interpretations were. Because of his insistence on a limitation of UN ends and means the Congo operation appeared to be plagued by three contradictions which I have discussed elsewhere.[43] There was a contradiction between the reality—one of civil war—and a principle which, even though it was derived from the Charter, nevertheless could only be a crippling fiction given the circumstances, i.e., the principle of nonintervention. There was another contradiction between the nature of the problem and the way in which the UN approached it, i.e., the concentration on the policing rather than on the political aspects, on the shibboleth of force rather than on the causes which led to its use. Such an emphasis resulted from the principle of nonintervention, but it had marked previous UN actions as well. It may have resulted from Mr. Hammarskjöld's own sense of priorities, but it can also be traced back to the Charter (where Chapter VII is informed by a sense of urgency entirely missing from Chapter VI). Finally, a contradiction existed between the stakes of the Congo conflict and the means at the disposal of the Organization.

I have tried earlier to show the inconveniences which resulted from the Secretary-General's approach. But it would be thoroughly unfair to condemn the effects without assessing the motives; and his reasons for his somewhat narrow and tortuous line cannot be dismissed lightly. Patrick O'Donovan has described him as a man who "compels himself to objectivity as priests do to prayer, and he binds himself by simply two laws: the UN Charter and the law of possibility."[44] By putting together various statements (and particularly those of the last annual report), I think one can derive the following arguments. First, the UN, in its mission, should respect its own basic principles; among those principles is that of nonintervention, which meant here that one had to let the Congolese "decide freely for themselves without any outside influences and with full knowledge of facts."[45] The implication clearly was drawn, in the Secretary-General's last two annual reports, that the Organization would destroy itself if it sacrificed its principles to expediency whenever it was not absolutely obliged to do so (as it was in areas, like Hungary, where it was quite without influence): "any result bought at the price of a compromise with the principles or ideals

---

[42] On April 15, 1961, a Guinean amendment aimed at deleting the words "by the Secretary-General" in one part of the seventeen-power draft was defeated by a vote of 83-11-5.

[43] See "An Evaluation of the UN," *Ohio State Law Journal*, Summer 1961 (Vol. 22, No. 3), p. 477-494.

[44] "The Precedent of the Congo," *International Affairs*, April 1961 (Vol. 37, No. 2), p. 181-188.

[45] See *International Organization*, Autumn 1961 (Vol. 15, No. 4), p. 561.

of the Organization . . . is bought at too high a price."[46] If the UN wanted
to preserve its authority, it simply could not become just the instrument of
shifting majorities, for it would then lose the support of the minorities. An
international organization, which is not a super-state, can deepen its authority and play its role only if it acts as an impartial force, not if it is merely
a weapon in the hands of blocs. Secondly, the UN had to remain modest
because, in the present conditions of the world, international organization is
particularly fragile; it simply does not have the means to be very ambitious,
and any policy which would expose the Organization beyond those means
would backfire. Also, the more ambitious its operation, the more it risks
becoming a stake in the power struggle. One can imagine how much UN
resources would have been taxed if it had had to step, not merely through
resolutions, into the Algerian war. These were precisely some of the reasons
which had led most Members tacitly to discard the collective security function of the UN.[47] In an explosive world, few nations are willing to let an
international soldier operate if they are not sure that this soldier fights their
battles. As long as such is the case, it is wiser to have the UN play the
role of honest broker, or of fireman. Dag Hammarskjöld's calculation was
that, so to speak, a minimal operation would get maximum support.

The trouble was that a minimal operation produced what looked like
maximum turmoil in the field, and that dissatisfaction with this state of
affairs resulted in minimal support. Mr. Hammarskjöld had feared that a
more daring approach would backfire. His cautious one backfired in three
ways. First, the Secretary-General, who was so deeply convinced of the
decisive importance of his office, exposed himself most dangerously. Any
Secretary-General who tries to be the spokesman of a still only virtual international community runs a number of risks. If he defines the "international
interest" in so impartial a way that it does not coincide with the interests
of any group, there will be a glaring gap between his constituents and himself, and he will be performing a solitary tightrope walk too far over the
ground; to change the metaphor, the "loneliness of the long-distance runner"
is a melancholy one. If he defines the international interest in such a way
that it coincides with the interests of some, this convergence of "supranational" and "international" calculations may destroy his usefulness on both
levels, since the opponents of his constituents will accuse him of partiality.
Finally, in both cases, any attempt at defining an international interest which
differs from their own will bring down on him the wrath of the Soviets;
they resent any chief executive who is more than a mere administrator, and

---

[46] "Introduction to the fifteenth Annual Report of the Secretary-General to the General Assembly,"
UN Review, October 1960 (Vol. 7, No. 4), p. 27.

[47] See I. L. Claude, Jr., "The UN and the Use of Force," *International Conciliation* (No. 532),
March 1961.

less than their ally, and they deny the possibility of impartiality anyhow.[48] Now, Mr. Hammarskjöld's pitfalls were the first—isolation—and, inevitably, the third. While he isolated himself from a deadlocked melee of former constituents, some of whom attacked him bitterly, the operational weaknesses of his doctrine, which I have discussed, isolated him at crucial moments from his representatives in the field: in both directions the transmission links were strained.

Next, Mr. Hammarskjöld's approach backfired for the UN operation as well. In New York, discontent with the turn of events produced the very political polarization and paralysis which he probably thought a more aggressive policy would provoke. This revealed that in any major crisis, whatever its approach, the UN could not avoid becoming a stake. Moreover, the Secretary-General's line made it a stake, but prevented it from being a very impressive force on the spot. There, ONUC was caught in the dead end I have mentioned. Its legal status reveals the inadequacy of the thread: since it was not a collective security operation, it required the consent of the host state; but precisely because it had to restrict itself to a much smaller task than the one the government of the host state wanted it to accomplish, it had to be able to stay there and operate (or abstain from operation) despite that government's hostility. It was the very emphasis on modesty of ends and means which led to an assertion of independence from the central government. It could not be the latter's arm; it had to be autonomous so as to be able often to be much less. The Secretary-General, halfway, so to speak, between the Korean and Suez precedents, chose to find a legal shelter in Articles 39 and 40.[49] But at the same time as he was proclaiming the duty of nonintervention, he stated that the UN task consisted of saving a drowning man even without his authorization.[50] Ambassador Dayal found that it was not easy to be both neutral and at the service of the central government. Neither in New York nor in the Congo did the policy of Mr. Hammarskjöld provide the necessary cooperation of the Members and of the host.

Finally, only to the extent to which the original ends and means were violated or transcended has some progress appeared in the Congo. The ban on force and on UN political intervention resulted only in violence. It is the combination a) of violence despite the ban (Lumumba's murder), b) of UN local violence leading to or resulting from a lifting of the ban (against

---

[48] See Michel Virally, "Vers une Réforme du Secrétariat des Nations Unies?" *International Organization*, Spring 1961 (Vol. 15, No. 2), p. 236–255.

[49] Statement to the Security Council, December 13, 1960. On this issue, see E. M. Miller, "Legal Aspects of the UN Action in the Congo," *American Journal of International Law*, January 1961 (Vol. 55, No. 1), p. 1–28; and Alan Karabus, "UN Activities in the Congo," *Proceedings of the American Society of International Law*, 1961, p. 30 ff.

[50] A/PV.906, October 17, 1960.

Katanga), and c) of political pressures exercised from the outside on the Congolese which have broken the deadlock of the first winter. Proudhon has written that force remains the law-maker in a whole series of cases, among which he listed the creation, absorption, and break-up of a nation.[51] Mr. Hammarskjöld's policy seemed to lead to an endless terror. The UN gradually opted for an end, even if mildly terrifying.

Good intentions, but results which disproved them—this is a harsh verdict. Indeed, it may well be too harsh. For we must consider now the *alternatives*. On the one hand, total UN abstention would probably have led to big power intervention at a much higher pitch of intensity, and possibly to another international brushfire conflict such as those of South East Asia, with incalculable effects on Africa. On the other hand, what could a stronger UN mandate have meant? In the first place, theoretically, it could have meant a genuine UN take-over, whether one called it trusteeship or full responsibility for law and order, as Ghana and Ceylon suggested it at times:[52] in other words, a finding that the Congo was not ready yet to use its premature independence. Thus it would have been the responsibility of the UN to exert that monopoly of the use of force which is the mark of sovereignty, to revive political life, and so on. But one sees at once that such a solution was a practical impossibility, not only because of the contradiction between such UN administration and the previous proclamation of Congo's independence, at a time when the winds of anticolonial change simply will not reverse themselves, but also because of a fundamental truth of which Mr. Hammarskjöld was deeply aware: the UN is not a kind of monolithic force capable of imposing its order on a domestic chaos. It is itself an arena and a stake. It is a battlefield of national and bloc forces. It is condemned to carry to the scene of domestic chaos its own chaos of individual interests and global incoherence, in General de Gaulle's words.[53] The relations between troubles in the Congo and troubles in the UN remind one of the complicated mirror games which embitter the two troupes of actors who perform, on two superposed levels, in Jean Genet's play, *The Blacks*. Mr. Hammarskjöld may have been wrong to believe that the more modest the mission, the more subdued the intra-UN clashes; but he was right to guess that the greater the responsibilities and the stakes, the bigger the peril. The definition by the UN of a Congo policy, at a time when Lumumba had split not only the Congo but the Organization itself, would have been practically impossible. Indeed, the deadlocks of the winter of 1960–1961 proved this.

In the second place, a stronger UN mandate could mean (and to a large extent means today) not a submission of the Congo to the UN, but a sub-

[51] *La Guerre et la Paix*, Vol. 1, Paris, E. Dentu, 1861.
[52] Notably in the Security Council debates of February 1961.
[53] See his press conference of April 11, 1961.

ordination of the UN to the central government of the Congo. But here there are problems and contradictions just as formidable as those which plagued Mr. Hammarskjöld's policy of an independent but limited ONUC.

First, the new mandate allows the UN to use force to further certain political objectives—for the first time since the fateful General Assembly resolution of October 7, 1950, on the unification of Korea. If I may quote myself,[54] the reason for not encouraging such a trend is that when there is no well-defined and sufficiently broad consensus on those objectives, such a UN operation is likely to impair the future usefulness of the UN. It reduces the willingness of nations to let the UN be the *deus ex machina* in emergencies. Whereas Mr. Hammarskjöld's policy reduced the effectiveness of the UN as a force so much that its mission became a stake, the opposite line risks making of its mission so much of a stake in the big power struggle that its effectiveness would be impaired. For the big powers may keep a certain detachment about peace forces, but they can hardly fail to be more worried, and therefore more involved, about shooting forces. Political efficiency is thus not assured, nor is military efficiency. For the forces at the disposal of the UN remain pitifully weak, and the Members have shown no willingness to accept even a permanent peace force. Should a shooting UN force be defeated, one can imagine what a setback it would be; but should it win and reach its objectives, the UN itself could be rocked by dissents and withdrawals. The pitfall which the acting Secretary-General must avoid is the second one I have listed: the pitfall of partiality.

Thus, the use of force by the UN to reach political goals in a collective security operation such as Korea made trouble, and more trouble could be expected, should the Korean precedent be repeated in circumstances in which aggression was less clear and the UN objectives were more controversial. But, secondly, the conditions of a civil war are even more ambiguous and dangerous for the UN. The resort to violence by an international organization in such circumstances takes on a very different meaning; for the use of an international force as a police force at the service of a government is a highly questionable precedent. In a world in which so many regimes are shaky, so many borders artificial, so many unions arbitrary, can the UN afford to serve as the secular arm, say, of a future Mali complaining about another Senegal secession? Here is the strength of Mr. Hammarskjöld's position: if one starts poking in domestic conflicts, where does one stop? In a world of glass houses, not too many bricks ought to be thrown, so that the interior of the houses can remain unrevealed. Insofar as we are all murderers, let us not call each other criminals—this is the precept which any attempt at defining aggressive war violates. Insofar as we are all potential Congos,

[54] "Popularity and Power in the UN," *New Leader*, February 19, 1962, p. 22–23.

should we be so enthusiastic about letting a weak government use a world force as its constabulary?

Finally, the example of the Congo today shows that ONUC cannot be simply an arm of the central government for the restoration of law and order. For insofar as law and order are still threatened by the lack of discipline in the government army, as U Thant has recognized, some margin of independent action must be preserved.[55] Consequently the risk of new disagreements with the local authorities as well is not ruled out.

Thus, the final lesson about the UN mission is that the world is too explosive either to live without an impartial fireman, or to turn him into an additional pyromaniac. But in circumstances of civil war, the world at large and the scene of the fire simply will not let the fireman do his job easily. Mr. Hammarskjöld's "preventive diplomacy" required, in order to be successful, a) firm support from his political constituents, i.e., both a tacit concert of the Great Powers and a consensus of those states which he saw as the main "clients" of the UN, and b) the cooperation of authorities on the spot. These were the conditions which had prevailed in previous crises, but which the Congo circumstances made largely impossible. The opposite policy, however, puts the UN into the position of acting not so much as a help to states, as if it were a state using force to reach political goals when peaceful solutions have failed. Consequently, instead of removing causes of tension and eliminating violence, it adds more trouble. Instead of an international Red Cross, there is one more army at work. The very broad definition of self defense in the second Katanga operation, in December 1961, reminds one of Robert W. Tucker's analyses of nations' hypocrisies or inconsistencies in the claim of self defense.[56] Furthermore, since the UN is neither a nation, nor a supranational agency endowed with compelling authority and force over nations, its action cannot help reflecting the conflicts among its Members[57] and the frailty (political and administrative) of its executive.

I would therefore conclude that in the present world, civil wars will be rough on the UN whatever policy it adopts. Since however the UN can often stay away from them only at too great a peril to itself and the world, it seems condemned to muddle through, case by case, in search of an all-too-

[55] See note 38.
[56] See Robert W. Tucker, *The Just War*, Baltimore, Johns Hopkins University Press, 1960. The reports of the officer-in-charge of UN operations explained that among ONUC objectives there was a very broad range of objectives in and around Elizabethville [see *UN Review*, January 1962 (Vol. 9, No. 1), p. 45 ff].
[57] One of the aspects of those conflicts is the slowness and heaviness of the procedure in New York: suggestions about good offices or any reorganization took weeks to mature. In the Security Council, invitations to non-members to present their viewpoints as interested parties also led to delays. As for the military and administrative weaknesses of the Secretariat, see the introduction to the fifteenth annual report, and my remarks above, p. 346–350.

breakable thread. In other circumstances the late Secretary-General's cautious policy is more appropriate to the present world.[58] Maybe he was too narrow in his policing, antiseptic, but not sufficiently political approach to disputes. For although he was willing to *send* a force to curb violence, he hesitated, as in the Suez crisis, to *use* a force to further certain political objectives. But he was, I think, justified in refusing to use *force* in order to reach them. Unfortunately, such a distinction is very hard to maintain in circumstances of civil chaos.

The behavior of the Members: A few remarks should be made about the attitude of the UN Members during the Congo crisis. Once again, we find that their approach to the UN is a purely instrumental or tactical one. When they think that the Organization can promote their interests, they are quite willing to strengthen its mandate. When they think their interests require that the local status quo be left to take care of itself, they see to it that the mandate remains unobtrusive. Thus, the United States, long respectful of the Congolese right to settle their own disputes, nevertheless pressed for (and obtained) UN "recognition" of Mr. Kasavubu. When the local situation became disturbing to US interests, the US supported first the limited strengthening of the mandate in February 1961, then the considerable shift of November. The USSR, unable to get either in the Security Council or in the General Assembly a majority to support its own policy—which would have made of ONUC first Lumumba's arm, then his liberator, and finally his avenger—nevertheless opposed resolutions (such as the seventeen-power draft in April 1961) which would have somewhat strengthened the UN mandate but in a direction contrary to Soviet interests.[59] Most of the Casablanca powers, having failed to get the Assembly to strengthen ONUC according to their desires, weakened it deliberately, since it was not serving their interests, by withdrawing from ONUC and from the Conciliation Commission. A number of delegates, favorable to Lumumba and to UN pressure on the Congolese designed to bring out the re-emergence of Lumumba as the leader, opposed the seating of Mr. Kasavubu in November 1961 under the pretext that such a move would hurt the process of conciliation in the Congo. Similarly, sovereignty is a catchword which can be used by all, with very different tactical meanings. To some of the former French African colonies, respect of the Congo's sovereignty means a strict policy of nonintervention; to Ghana, Guinea, or Mali it means a thorough decolonization and the rejection of "fake" independence.

If we turn to *the two main powers,* we reach certain conclusions which are mildly surprising. On the one hand, the Soviet Union has been, on

[58] See Michel Virally, *L'ONU,* Paris, Ed. du Seuil, 1961.
[59] Similarly in November 1961 the Soviets voted against a United States proposal which would have authorized the Secretary-General to assist the central government in the reorganization of Congolese armed units—the kind of measure which the Soviets advocated some months earlier.

the whole, rather isolated. In the Security Council, at first the Soviets did not dare to oppose an operation sponsored by Tunisia and Ceylon. When they used their veto against a draft which outlawed bilateral military aid to the central government, they found themselves alone in opposing the same text in the special session of the Assembly. The only draft they presented themselves in the Assembly (April 1961) not only did not go much beyond the seventeen-power draft which the Assembly endorsed, but even then received the support of only seventeen African and Asian states, while fifteen abstained and fourteen voted against it. They never submitted to the Assembly their plan of February 1961 for the dismissal of the Secretary-General and for termination of the UN operation within one month. In their suspicion of any UN undertaking which did not serve their own policy they were in a way closer to the more "conservative" states—such as those ex-French colonies which joined them in opposing the seventeen-power draft in April—than to the Casablanca powers, whose Congo policies largely coincided with Soviet desires but who would have liked the UN to turn over the responsibility for enforcing those policies to a kind of African command and peace force, with the exclusion of anyone else, particularly the Great Powers. In the Congo, the period of spectacular Soviet intervention was brief—the last two weeks of Mr. Lumumba's tenure as premier. Subsequently, Soviet activities were confined to recognition of, and political advice to, Mr. Gizenga.

On the other hand, the United States has, on the whole, succeeded rather well in either getting its own views endorsed by the General Assembly (e.g., the seating of Mr. Kasavubu) or reconciling its views and those of a large number of Africans and Asians. The only difficult period was the winter of 1960–1961. Such important steps as the original three resolutions, the seating of Mr. Kasavubu, the Security Council shift in February 1961, and the new policy of November 1961, were all endorsed by the United States. The Assembly votes of November and December 1960 showed a split between most of the Africans and Asians and the United States, but Lumumba's death narrowed the gap and produced the shifts in votes I have mentioned. Whether the US decision in November 1961 to support the resolution submitted by Ceylon, Liberia, and the UAR was ultimately in the US interest is a matter of domestic debate. What matters here is that it was not resisted by the United States, and that US policy makers decided it was in the national interest to support Mr. Adoula.[60]

Thus it is true that, at some of the crucial stages in the Security Council, the Soviets and the Americans found themselves either voting together (resolutions of July and August 1960 and November 1961) or not voting

[60] See George W. Ball, "The Elements of Our Congo Policy," Department of State Publication 7326, December 1961.

against one another (February 1961). This conjunction reflected the need for both superpowers to court and coax the "Third World" rather than to coerce and constrain it. But it is also true that, on the whole, and until now at least, it is the Soviet Union which has lost its gamble and the United States which has to a considerable extent succeeded. Of course, success has come precisely because US objectives were limited: a neutral Congo, not an ally. And, as shown by recent events, the creation of such a neutral Congo may even require the crushing of the most publicly pro-Western faction, in Katanga. However, Ambassador Stevenson's idea of the coincidence of US and UN interests,[61] and Mr. Ball's demonstration that "the UN is in the Congo with objectives that . . . parallel our own" are not false. To American right-wing critics, such a parallel only shows that the United States defines its objectives and interests in too "soft" a way. But to the Soviets, this seems little consolation for the emergence of a non-communist state, in which Lumumba is dead, Gizenga ousted, and Tshombé—indubitably a boon to extreme nationalists—something of an outcast. To the considerable extent to which Dag Hammarskjöld's definition of preventive diplomacy has facilitated such a conciliation of US and new nations' interests, the Soviets could not fail to see in the UN an American instrument and in the Secretary-General a Western stooge even though he was obviously moved more by principles than by "power bloc" calculations. Their frustrations in the Congo fed their attack on Mr. Hammarskjöld. As Daniel Cheever has suggested,[62] United States reliance on the Secretary-General to reach objectives consonant with US interests, flexibly defined, has seriously exposed the Secretary-General. It will be interesting to see whether Mr. Hammarskjöld's successor will be capable of acquiring at least Soviet neutrality, without supporting such policies as would reduce US enthusiasm for the UN and complicate US conciliation with the new states' interests.

For if we turn to the attitudes of *the new states,* we find that the so-called African-Asian bloc is so complex, and alignments within so un-frozen, that the way in which these states divide is far from determined. Much depends on the events, of course, but also on the kind of leadership provided both by the Secretary-General and by the United States. A fine analysis by Robert Good[63] has shown that, on the whole, the new states can be divided among "conservatives," "moderates," and "radicals." But two remarks must be added. First, none of those sub-groups has been monolithic. Thus, among the "conservatives," the vote of April 17, 1961, showed that some, like Sene-

[61] Quoted by Alexander Dallin, "The Soviet View of the UN," *International Organization,* Winter 1962 (Vol. 16, No. 1), p. 36.
[62] See Andrew Gyorgy and Hubert S. Gibbs, eds., *Problems in International Relations,* revised edition to be published by Prentiss-Hall in July 1962.
[63] "Congo Crisis: The Role of the New States," in *Neutralism,* Washington, D. C., Center of Foreign Policy Research, 1961.

gal, were less conservative than others. Among the moderates, some, like Ceylon and India, evolved in the direction of the radicals. Others, such as Tunisia, remained more favorable to a policy of nonintervention. Still others, such as Togo and Nigeria, passed through a "radical" phase during the winter, and left it when Lumumba disappeared.[64] Among the radicals, there remained throughout a difference between states such as Guinea or Mali, which not only withdrew their troops but also attacked the Secretary-General in violent terms, and Ghana, which criticized his policies and proposed an African substitute expedition but never broke with him nor withdrew its troops. Secondly, and consequently, it becomes obvious that the opportunities for political maneuver are considerable. In the circumstances of November–December 1960, too narrow an interpretation by the Secretary-General and too strong a United States support for one of the local contenders produced a deadlock in which a US and British resolution received the support of only eight African and Asian states.[65] In April 1961, a less restrictive interpretation, endorsed by the United States, was backed by 25 of the nations of Africa and Asia.[66] It is clear that no procolonial stand has a chance of being accepted either in the Security Council or in the General Assembly. But the gamut of possible anticolonialisms is still extremely wide.

If this is, in a way, a reassuring conclusion after too many depressing ones, there remains however one very dark spot. There is, almost everywhere, a widening gap between what nations expect the UN to do for them and what they are willing to do for the UN. It is true that they have tended to blame the Secretary-General for carrying out the mandate which they had either given him, or failed to modify. As he reminded them, "this is your operation, gentlemen."[67] But the financial difficulties of the UN, which result in so large a part from the Congo crisis, have pointed out more clearly and more cruelly than ever that international organization is an ambiguous halfway house which is asked to look as if it were a force of its own while embodying all the conflicts and inhibitions of a fragmented world. Consequently, whoever serves as such an organization's executive head is performing the thankless, indispensable, and suicidal task of a "Pope without a Church"[68] trying to realize as much of the Charter ideal as the nations will allow, in a world whose secular religions are locked in battle, whose realities turn ideals into weapons, and weapons into the most final of all final solutions.

---

[64] See note 31.
[65] The two-power draft, on December 20, 1960, received 43 votes in favor, among which were those of Malaya, Iran, Laos, China, Japan, the Philippines, Thailand, and Pakistan.
[66] See note 31.
[67] A/PV.871, September 26, 1960.
[68] Herbert Nicholas, "United Nations?" *Encounter*, January 1962, p. 8.

THE UNITED NATIONS AND THE PROBLEM OF AFRICAN DEVELOPMENT

Paul-Marc Henry

The United Nations is now playing a key role in the economic and technical development of the African continent and will undoubtedly be called upon to assume an even greater responsibility in this field during the next ten years. This development was correctly forecast five years ago by the late Secretary-General Dag Hammarskjöld. For he saw that the transition from the colonial era, which had made the European countries directly responsible for the development of the vast majority of the territories and peoples in Africa, prior to independence, would thrust upon the United Nations a very specific burden. As it happened, the question of the Congo has overshadowed the other aspects of UN activity in Africa, although one can note a remarkable continuity in the progressive implementation of a coordinated program where all agencies of the United Nations family have to play their part.

I. The General Picture of UN Activity and Assistance in Africa

The United Nations Economic Commission for Africa came into existence in 1958 with headquarters in Addis Ababa. Twenty-nine African states are at present members of the Commission together with five European states that have responsibilities in Africa. In addition, the Commission includes associate members whose political status is not yet determined. The Commission addresses itself to all the fields directly related to programs of African development as a whole. It has already been active in the field of training, in the programing and organizing of technical assistance, in the study of the flow of international aid to Africa, in the improvement of development planning techniques, and in the survey of trade and commodity, agriculture, statistics, industrial transport, and social problems. This has resulted in the Commission's keeping under virtually constant review the problems of the African continent as a whole.

Specialized agencies have established regional offices in Accra (FAO), in Lagos (ILO), in Brazzaville (WHO), in Cairo (FAO, ICAO), and in Alexandria (WHO) in addition to several area offices (Rabat, Dakar, Lagos,

PAUL-MARC HENRY is the former Secretary-General of the Commission for Technical Cooperation in Africa South of the Sahara (CCTA) and the Scientific Council for Africa South of the Sahara (CSA), and has had long experience in Africa. He is currently Associate Director of Operations of the United Nations Special Fund.

Brazzaville, Kampala, Nairobi, Addis Ababa, Cairo, and Tunis). Resident representatives of the Technical Assistance Board (who are also Directors of Special Fund programs) have been appointed at Rabat, Dakar, Monrovia, Accra, Abidjan, Lome, Lagos, Libreville, Leopoldville, Dar-es-Salaam, Tananarive, Mogadiscio, Addis Ababa, Khartoum, Cairo, Tripoli, and Tunis. This is no doubt an impressive network which makes it possible for practically every African country to have direct access to the vast pool of knowledge accumulated by the United Nations family during fifteen years of activity in all parts of the world.

It might be worth noting that the final control of such assistance is vested in the UN General Assembly and in the governing bodies of the Special Fund and the specialized agencies where African governments are fully represented and can exercise a decisive influence on the shaping and orientation of a program from which they wish to benefit.

The following figures indicate the extent to which the United Nations has been rendering assistance to Africa:[1]

SUMMARY OF ACTIVITIES IN AFRICA

UN Expanded Program of TA (Two years 1961–1962)		*United Nations Special Fund* (Total of projects since 1959)	
Cost of projects (in million $)	20.1	Number of projects	53
Number of experts	1,632	Cost of projects (in million $)	42.5
Number of fellowships	1,618		

Regular UN Technical Assistance Programs
(for two years 1961–1962)

	(in million $)
Regular Program in Economic Development	2.1
Advisory Social Services	1.2
Public Administration	0.8
OPEX (Operational, Administrative and Executive Personnel)	0.5
Total	4.6

Africa now ranks first among the five regions of the world receiving United Nations aid. Of the United Nations global technical assistance, some 30 percent has been allocated to Africa for the two-year period 1961–1962; and of the UN Special Fund's pre-investment projects approved so far, a full one-third in value is to be carried out in Africa.

Every specialized agency and the United Nations itself, acting through the technical assistance programs or as executing agencies for the UN Spe-

[1] "The United Nations and Africa—A Collection of Basic Information on the Economic and Social Activities of the United Nations and Related Agencies in Africa," UN Office of Public Information, February 1962.

cial Fund, as well as the Economic Commission for Africa, have all paid special attention to requirements of African countries. The International Bank for Reconstruction and Development, since 1951, has lent $891.7 million to Africa, not including the recent loan to Ghana, distributed as follows:

(In millions of U.S. dollars)

Algeria and Sahara	$ 60.0	Kenya	$ 14.0
Congo (Leopoldville)	120.0	Mauritania	66.0
East Africa	24.0	Nigeria	28.0
Ethiopia	25.5	Ruanda-Urundi	4.8
Federation of Rhodesia and		South Africa	221.8
Nyasaland	146.6	Sudan	74.0
French West Africa	7.1	Uganda	8.4
Gabon	35.0	United Arab Republic	56.5

Economic survey missions have been sent by the International Bank to Tanganyika, Nigeria, and Kenya. The International Development Association has extended a development credit of $13 million to the Sudan in its first transaction undertaken jointly with the International Bank.

In May 1961 a meeting organized by the UN Educational, Scientific, and Cultural Organization (UNESCO) and the UN Economic Commission for Africa in Addis Ababa launched a program for education of over $11.5 million for 1961–1962. This emergency program covers school buildings, instruction for teachers, technological training, etc. The spectacular achievements of WHO and UNICEF, in cooperation with the existing health services, in attacking basic health problems such as malaria, yaws, leprosy, tuberculosis, worm infestations, onchocerciasis, sleeping sickness, and malnutrition, are well known. Over and above the activities of the specialized agencies, one cannot fail to mention the United Nations emergency action in the Congo where civilian operations are gathering increasing importance.

This picture of multilateral assistance augurs well for the future of United Nations action in Africa. It remains to be seen, however, whether this effort is sufficient or not, and whether the regional approach is not hiding some of the basic problems with which African countries will still be faced even if assistance were to be multiplied many times and if political problems were not to act as a deterrent rather than a stimulus during the next few years.

II. The Political Background

In the special issue on Africa of the *Technical Assistance Newsletter,* dated June–July 1961, it was remarked that: "As of 30 June 1961, there were a total of 26 African States, with some 190,000,000 people belonging to the United Nations. The date cannot be omitted from a statement of this kind, because the pace on that continent turns current events into history in less than a year."

Indeed, since June 1961 the pace of events has accelerated. The colonial powers have all but lost their grip on the African continent. Angola, Mozambique, and the Federation of Rhodesia-Nyasaland are being progressively, and so it seems irresistibly, sucked into the whirlpool of Pan-Africanism and anticolonialism. The Union of South Africa is bracing itself against the coming impact of these new forces which are working feverishly toward its political and economic isolation.

Once it is said that the former metropolitan powers have all but left Africa, it must also be noted that from the point of view of aggregate figures the main source of financial, technical, and commercial support to the new African states still comes from those powers within the framework of systems of technical and financial assistance. This support is closely conditioned by previous relationships and is highly sensitive to political and even sentimental factors.

So much has been said about this sudden acceleration of the pace of events in Africa, however, that the sense of perspective is apt to be blurred. The fact that modern means of communications have broken for good the isolation even of the most remote parts, making it possible for a modern traveler to go across the continent in practically no time, is the source of a misleading impression that the same time factor is no longer relevant to the analysis of the evolution of the various African communities.

One should not forget that speed and acceleration may be only relative factors in the present African conditions where political considerations are perhaps as important as measurable economic and financial elements, although they are much more difficult to analyze, let alone to forecast. In other words, technical and economic assistance to emerging Africa is as much a political problem as an economic one, and in addition, raises complex questions of methods, tactics and long-term strategy.

III. The Specific Needs of Africa

There is a prevailing tendency to think that Africa will be the problem child of the period 1961–1971, the UN "Development Decade." It is expected that many countries in Asia and Latin America will have reached by then the so-called "take-off stage," if they have not already done so. Western Europe, the United States, and Japan, as well as Eastern Europe and the USSR, will have moved far ahead of their present standard of living and economic achievements (if we are to accept their own proposed rate of growth as realistic). China is tackling with energy the exceptional problem of overpopulation and unbalance between industry and agriculture.

In the meantime, most of the African countries are relegated implicitly or explicitly to the preparatory stages of economic development—that is, to an inventory of natural resources and training of human resources, and their immediate prospects of developing a sufficient rate of domestic capital formation or of international investment are often rated as poor.

The question of estimating the needs of Africa as a whole or of the African countries individually is one of the most elusive of exercises. One must clearly distinguish between:

a) those countries which can afford to pay for the normal apparatus of government out of their present resources and at the same time to satisfy with little or no foreign assistance the basic needs of their citizens in the fields of public administration, public health, agricultural services, and education, and which enjoy an adequate system of communications;

b) those countries which do not yet possess this apparatus, but have a reasonable expectation of reaching these minimum standards in a relatively short time; and,

c) those countries which are now receiving direct or indirect subsidies without which the machinery of government would have to be drastically reduced and which present hardly any expectation of short-term economic development on a sufficient scale.

The brutal fact is that without some permanent connection with external sources of finance and administrative "know-how" through existing bilateral channels, or other machinery yet to be created, vast areas of Africa run the risk of a crippling paralysis which no amount of technical assistance or welfare work can expect to counteract. This is vividly demonstrated in the case of the former Belgian Congo where the minimum machinery of administration is being maintained with the assistance of the United Nations at a relatively high cost to the international community, which does not seem to be prepared to pay for it on a long-term basis (at the end of 1961, $35 million had been pledged to the United Nations Fund for the Congo, contrasted with the original goal of $100 million).

IV. A Problem of Transition from Bilateral to Multilateral Aid

In 1960, bilateral aid to Africa, which covers the various kinds of public expenditures including direct subsidies to keep the machinery of government going, was almost ten times as large as multilateral aid; that is, $1,227 million against $146 million, out of which $130 million came from the International Bank. In other words, just to maintain the present level of assistance presupposes that:

a) either the former metropolitan powers will continue their present level of assistance (which includes the provision of personnel as well as financial subsidies), or

b) other world powers will take some of the burden—which means that the United States and the Soviet Union will engage in a large-scale policy of grants or interest-free loans, or

c) that international agencies will have to take over the predominantly bilateral systems of assistance and to channel corresponding amounts to African countries.

In addition, it is well known that the capital requirements (public or private) to expand transportation, to develop natural resources, and to train human potential in order to induce self-sustained growth are several times as high as the present annual inflow, which is estimated in the neighborhood of $1,400 million for public capital and $500 million for private capital.[2]

There is little doubt as to the desire of the receiving countries to see a greater amount and proportion of aid channeled through a multilateral system of one sort or another under United Nations sponsorship. African countries now represent a most important element in the composition of the General Assembly. Their aggregate voting power makes them the most significant of all regional groupings. In fact, this political position is the only effective weapon at their disposal in a world-wide bargaining for the redistribution of the economic, financial, and technical surpluses produced by the most advanced countries. Other levels of bargaining and negotiations exist within special systems, such as the French Community, the British Commonwealth, and the European Common Market, but it is safe to assume that in the last analysis the African countries as a whole, while taking advantage of specific groupings, will place greater emphasis on the world community as represented in the United Nations General Assembly.

This means that efforts will be made to re-channel through already existing (IBRD, IDA) or proposed (United Nations Capital Development Fund) international financial institutions most of the financial and technical assistance now flowing through bilateral channels. Conversely, the major donor countries (United States, United Kingdom, Common Market members, and Eastern bloc countries) will be forced into an "agonizing reappraisal" of the amount, duration, and final administration of the capital and technical "know-how" they are willing to put at the disposal of the African nations.

The net result of this reorganization may very well be a net decrease in the aggregate volume of aid received by Africa and not the expected increase. In other words, while the United Nations family will have to assume

[2] *Op. cit.*

a greater share of the total burden of assistance to Africa, it may well be faced with increased needs which will make its own assistance appear grossly inadequate. The Congo is an example of this dilemma. A word of warning has already been sounded—during the recent debate on Ruanda-Urundi —on the continuous responsibility of former colonial or trustee powers toward the new nations of Africa.

V. The Nature of Aid

Leaving aside for one moment the difficult problems of the channeling of aid, and even of its volume, let us turn to the question of its nature and its objective, as well as to the delicate issue of the "absorptive capacity" of Africa for aid.

African needs point clearly to the necessity for the next ten years of a continuous movement of experts to the continent, with more and more emphasis placed on the level and the quality of expert advisers, together with a vast effort in the direction of general education and of specialized training in the field. The question immediately arises of the capacity of the developed world to provide the great number of experts needed in the various fields concerned—which range all the way from agriculture to industry and which include the areas of primary, secondary, university, and technical education, as well as all fields related to technological development. Individual governments and the UN specialized agencies are encountering more and more difficulties in recruiting the right kind of experts and educators. African governments have to pay higher wages to expatriates. At the same time, there are disturbing signs that some of the well-trained Africans are not employed as they should be, and that there is already some waste of skilled manpower. It is by no means certain that African nations will not be faced with the same problem as some Latin American and Asian nations, i.e., that their own technicians tend to be absorbed by the developing countries or by the international organizations themselves.

In addition, during the transition period a most pressing problem will prevail with respect to the taking over of pre-existing technical and administrative structures for which skilled personnel of local origin is not immediately available. While the political machinery of government can be transferred without too much difficulty and, indeed, has functioned much better after independence than many expected, the shortage of staff in all technical departments is obvious in practically every country of Africa, and especially at the intermediate level.

VI. A Problem of Costs and Absorptive Capacity

Much has been done and more will be done by the United Nations and other sources of assistance to alleviate this difficulty, but little has been said or done about the problem of *initial cost,* i.e., investment in training, and *recurrent expenditures,* i.e., level of salaries of government employees compared with local resources.

It may seem paradoxical, but it is realistic to assume that Africa will have to mobilize fully its own economic resources at the expense of savings and investment to be able to afford the cost of the administrative and technical apparatus without which no development and sustained growth are possible. No amount of technical and financial assistance from the outside, through the United Nations or bilateral channels, can substitute for this. Indeed, the most explosive situation could be created if trained personnel of local origin were made available (and there are reasons to believe that it is possible to train the necessary number during the next decade) and could not be utilized by their own country because of the low level of economic activities of the country taken as a whole, and the resulting low level of public expenditures.

This problem is clearly summarized in the following quotation from the *Technical Assistance Newsletter:*[3]

> The absorptive capacity of most African countries is limited in the first instance by their lack of trained manpower, both to work on government development schemes and to work alongside international experts. Faced with this situation, the governments have wisely put a top priority on those technical assistance projects which are of a training nature. But training has its own potential frustrations and its own problem of absorption. What Africa *needs* in the way of manpower, it may not be able to *use.*
>
> An FAO official said recently that 250 veterinarians would have to be graduated for each of the next several years to assure a decent livestock industry and to replace the Europeans who are leaving. But if the schools were established and this number trained annually, the various governments probably could not afford to employ all of them, for reasons which include the low standard of livestock and their poor economic return.

Closer attention should certainly be paid to this problem, particularly to its financial aspects, by the international agencies as well as the governments directly concerned. UNESCO, which is setting up its own system of economic evaluation of the cost of training and education, has shown a clear awareness of the problem of absorption. Likewise, the International Labor Organization (ILO) has revealed its understanding of the problem from another angle, i.e., that of employment or unemployment of potential man-

[3] *Technical Assistance Newsletter,* June–July 1961, p. 16.

power. Indeed, experiences derived from other parts of the world seem to show that it is only at the highest level of economic development that the integration in the general economy of trained personnel does not constitute a major social and political question.

Examples abound of countries in Asia and in Latin America where the underemployment of "intellectuals" (which may include technically trained personnel as well as the so-called "lawyers") has not been solved and is at the root of unrest and instability.

This is not to say that training should be carefully measured like a potent medicine. No country in Africa will accept an approach to education and technical training whereby training would be strictly proportioned to economic prospects which would themselves be conditioned by a problematic reorientation of the flow of public and private investment toward Africa.

VII. The Responsibility of the UN Family

In this connection, the United Nations family has accepted a very special kind of responsibility. Through the definition of world-wide minimum standards in the fields of health, education, vocational training, agricultural practices, productivity, industrial development, among others, it has contributed more than any bilateral or joint agency to the acceptance by African governments of a particular line of policy and the attainment of certain objectives to which they are now firmly committed. The UN family has also undertaken to assist these African nations in going one step further by giving an acceptable social and economic content to their newly-won independence.

Let us now examine briefly how far Africa, in close association with the United Nations, can move *on the road to self-help through mobilizing its own actual and potential resources.*

The essential dependence of the African economy on the eve of the "Decade of Development" is aptly expressed in the following extract from the introduction which Mekki Abbas, Executive Secretary of the United Nations Economic Commission for Africa, has written in the report "The United Nations and Africa:"

> Unless political independence leads to real improvement in the standard of life of the African peoples, the frustration of the rising expectations of the justifiably impatient masses may lead to political instability in many parts of Africa. This is the challenge which faces most African leaders, and this is the problem which all of them are determined to tackle in order to consolidate their countries' political autonomy and achieve economic independence.
>
> The most effective long-term solution to the problem of inadequate and unstable earnings from the export of primary commodities, however, is the diversification of

the exports of the African countries and particularly the development of manufacturing industries, not only for domestic markets but also for export. In this connection, intra-African trade offers considerable possibilities given proper co-ordination and planning. African industrialization must be conceived of not merely in terms of the simple processing of raw materials previously exported in the crude form, but must also involve the whole process of the development and diversification of an industrial base. Again industrialization for Africa cannot usefully be limited only to the production of consumer goods either for the domestic market or for export; it should also embrace the development of capital goods industries, based on each country's resource endowment, which can meet in part at least the domestic demand for investment goods.

The systematic pursuit of this type of regional approach to the major problems of African development is apt in itself to produce two kinds of reactions. On the one hand, it can reinforce the feeling of grievance and frustration among those poorly-endowed nations which have been led to believe that political independence of individual national units as such is the primary key to economic development. On the other, it can suggest to certain African nations the idea of shielding themselves from the consequences of the widespread factors of depression through arrangements for protected markets or through special sources of finance. The latter attitude, and the reactions that it provokes in other governments, is exemplified in the present debate on the effect of the Common Market policy on the African economy.

It seems that the only long-term solution to the problem of the relative sluggishness of African development lies not only in regional cooperation but also in a dramatic increase of Africa's share in the world production of agricultural as well as industrial commodities. It is true that relevant market factors are holding down African producers and delaying the time when their potential wealth can be developed. This is clearly the case with those primary products that tropical Africa is trying to sell on the world market. It is likewise true concerning the development of hydroelectric potential such as the Congo, the Nile, and other major African rivers, and of major mineral deposits such as iron and bauxite, with some encouraging exceptions. Unless the world community organizes itself to give the actual and potential African producers a fair chance to participate in the increasing prosperity of its most developed parts, Africa will be faced with an economic and political "impasse" that no amount of technical and financial stopgap assistance can alter.

The Special Fund of the United Nations is entrusted with a specific responsibility in this area. Its main duty consists of assisting the developing countries in all pre-investment activities relating to their natural and human resources. During the next few years the Special Fund will inevitably be faced with pressing requests from the African countries for a systematic assessment in technical and economic terms of their potential mineral and hydrological resources, let alone petitions for assistance in the field of applied research and technical training. All these requests will be presented by governments which have in mind the pressing need for diversification of existing production and the discovery of new materials for export and raw materials for local industrialization derived from the development of their own power potential. In other words, the basic goal of industrialization and increased economic independence will stimulate all African governments in their quest for technical assistance and advisory services and, in due course, for their necessary financing.

Through its insistence on counterpart contributions in the form of cash or services, the Special Fund is bound to make the governments more conscious of the need for a total mobilization of their own limited resources. Alternatively, it may also make them painfully aware of their own relative inadequacy in the field of trained personnel and normal finance.

The truth cannot be escaped that the only road to maturity in the field of economic thinking lies through this painful process. Only the United Nations is in a position to stress the need for careful husbanding of available resources and long-term planning. Coming from any other group of states, such a suggestion would look like another disguised attempt to maintain Africa in the ranks of the dependent regions of the world, which it has held for too long. Through their membership at the United Nations, the African countries have a possibility and indeed a right to watch the process of redistribution of world resources and see that they get their rightful share, on the condition that they act as responsible members of the world community.

VIII. Conclusions

The basic factors and objectives of United Nations activities in Africa during the next ten years can be summed up as follows:

a) The United Nations will have to accept an increased share of direct responsibility in the field of technical assistance, which will include in many cases the taking over of responsibilities previously assumed by metropolitan powers, without necessarily being given adequate financial means to do so.

b) The African nations will be caught increasingly in the dilemma of additional recurrent expenditures for the maintenance of basic administrative and technical services at the expense of their capacity to save and invest in long-term projects.

c) Unless there is a spectacular rise in the level of economic activities, African countries will find it more and more difficult to absorb their own trained people, let alone engage in profitable employment their increased population.

d) There is an over-all risk of heightened dependence of the African economy vis-à-vis the rest of the world.

e) The international financial institutions are, as yet, not in a position to satisfy all the basic requirements in capital investment which are indispensable prerequisites for self-sustained growth.

f) The United Nations has assumed a special responsibility in defining world-wide standards which have been accepted as national objectives by African countries. It has also undertaken the specific responsibility of assisting the African countries to inventory their natural resources.

In the last analysis, the United Nations is the only organization through which the problem of the development of Africa can be discussed in a world-wide context. Africa cannot be treated in isolation. The development of its natural resources and the adequacy of economic returns for its primary products, as well as its own internal development, call for a world-wide understanding. Limited arrangements or special political and economic connections at present play an essential part in keeping the new nations going. But they are at best in the nature of stopgap arrangements and do not solve the problem of capital investment. The African governments have a right to ask for long-term measures which would guarantee that over a period of years their essential economic and technical dependence will be turned into a normal partnership on equal terms. They have a right to ask for assistance which would not penalize them for being late-comers on the road to independence and development. They have a right to ask from the United Nations family unreserved assistance in the assessment of their natural resources so that they can use this knowledge as the basis for fair negotiations with the rest of the world.

Economically developed countries and countries on the road to development which benefit from the exploitation of the existing resources have an obligation to assist the African continent as well as other areas of the world during their transitional period of development. However, some dangerous trends appear which may make the more generous potential donors and investors wary of orienting their resources toward the African continent. A serious process of disinvestment is actually taking place in numerous parts of Africa where the European entrepreneur was the largest contributor to self-sustained economic activities. Increased resources are obviously needed in all fields of financial and technical assistance at a time when the present system of normal assessment and special voluntary contributions shows signs of fatigue on the international level. If we accept the contention that Africa is basically rich in underdeveloped potential, natural and human, the most advanced nations in the world should place their trust in the final result of this development potential. Even from the point of view of their long-term interest as major consumers of basic raw materials, they have to accept the idea that their assistance is in the nature of an insurance policy, not against any specific political evil, but in favor of the solidarity between nations. A system has to be found whereby potential resources would be considered as bankable assets and aid would be requested on the basis of economic expectations.

After ten years of technical assistance experience all over the world, including Africa, and at a time when the UN has accepted new responsibilities toward the recently independent African nations, there is little doubt that the stage is set for a bold new·conception of African development in which all the UN family will have to play its part with the full support of those countries which have already achieved substantial economic advancement.

AFRICA AT THE UN: SOME OBSERVATIONS

John H. Spencer

Within the space of less than six years, the African membership in the United Nations has increased from three to twenty-eight Members constituting the largest geographical group in the Organization.[1] Furthermore, as many as seven other territories may become independent and seek membership before the end of 1965.

I. The Rise of the African Presence—Formation of the African Caucus

This sudden and massive incursion of African states into the World Organization has naturally aroused curiosity concerning the role of these states within the United Nations and speculation with respect to their effect upon its functioning.

The African states can today amass, when they are fully united, some 26 percent of the votes in the General Assembly. Although this is not equivalent to the 39 percent position which the Latin American states had in the early years of the United Nations, it is nevertheless a major bloc of votes capable of exercising a pervasive effect upon Assembly proceedings. Over and beyond the mere votes alone, which thus far have often been widely divided save on clear-cut anticolonialist questions and certain broad matters in the realm of peace and security, the operation of the African caucus functioning in collaboration with the larger Afro-Asian caucus has become one of the principal factors in General Assembly politics.

The African caucus may be said to date from the establishment of an "informal working machinery" at the UN initiated by the First Conference of Independent African States meeting at Accra in 1958. It was only after the admission of the large number of new African states in 1960, however, and the eruption of the Congo crisis, that the caucus became a major force in UN politics. As the Congo situation developed the African Members became both increasingly vocal and dexterous in political maneuvering. One measure of their influence was seen in their insistence upon the Secretary-General's accepting an Afro-Asian consultation committee on Congo affairs. Another was the vote taken at their demand on October 11, 1961, to cen-

JOHN H. SPENCER is Professor of International Law and Diplomacy at the Fletcher School of Law and Diplomacy. From 1943–1961 he was Senior Adviser in Foreign Affairs to the Ethiopian government.

[1] South Africa, which is not in the African caucus, is excluded for the purposes of this study.

sure the South African delegate for remarks in the General Assembly. On this occasion the African position resulted in a favorable vote of 67 to 1, with 36 states abstaining or "not participating." This was a vast change from a decade earlier when the General Assembly had at one point selected the Union of South Africa, over objections of the African states, as the representative of that continent to help achieve a solution of the Eritrea situation.

By combining their forces with the Asian states in the Afro-Asian caucus, which when united commands 47 percent of the Assembly vote, the African states have been able to increase even further their leverage in the proceedings of the General Assembly.

II. African Stands on Some Issues before the General Assembly

Space does not permit a detailed review of the positions which the African states have taken in the multiplicity of votes before the General Assembly. Their stands have varied from time to time, depending upon circumstances, upon the type of question before the Assembly, and upon political influences of many kinds operating both within the group and upon its members from other sources. The record shows that most of the African states voted more or less closely with the Western powers on a wide range of issues when they first became independent. As time has passed group pressures, anticolonialist sentiments, desires to demonstrate complete independence, and an "African view," as well as suasion by external arguments and blandishments, have led many of the states to part company with the Western delegations and to vote differently.

In glancing back over the record one can discern certain broad patterns of voting on colonial issues, as distinguished from questions involving the East-West struggle and from what might be termed "other questions" where neither colonial nor Cold War elements were at work.

Questions of "colonialism" are quite understandably capable of evoking a heated, emphatic, and vigorous show of strength against what is identified as the colonialist policy or action. This has been particularly evident where the action has related directly to African territory, as in the case of Portuguese Angola, or French evacuation from the Bizerta base in Tunisia. On the resolution at the fifteenth session calling for early termination of colonial rule generally, the African states spoke with a common voice. On the Algerian situation, on the other hand, the African states found it impossible to speak with a single voice or purpose. At the fifteenth session some of them, notably the members of the leftist and politically aggressive Casablanca grouping of states, including Ghana, Guinea, Mali, Morocco, and the United Arab Republic, bitterly condemned French policy and pressed hard for a resolution demanding a UN-supervised plebiscite in Algeria. Other states, especially those in the Brazzaville grouping of former French dependencies, were disposed, because of their associations with France, to resist such moves in opposition to the Casablanca grouping, while still others, identified with neither grouping, abstained, were absent, or voted on opposite sides.

The same transpired at the sixteenth session on the resolution calling for the neutralization of Africa with respect to nuclear testing. Most of the Brazzaville grouping abstained with France in the balloting.

On issues closely related to the Cold War, divisions have occurred among the African Members. Some have inclined to move progressively in the direction of an Eastward orientation, lining up their votes time and again with the Soviet bloc. This has been particularly characteristic of the Casablanca grouping. However, in such questions as disarmament, Tibet, Hungary, Cuba, and indeed, even on the Congo, the Casablanca group has not presented a united front. And one can even see tendencies on the part of such states as Liberia, Libya, the Sudan, and Ethiopia, which had previously been generally friendly toward the West, to cast their votes for Soviet-favored proposals, as in certain resolutions on summit talks, the Congo, and Cuba. On the other hand, members of both the Brazzaville and the Monrovia groupings have on many occasions voted in substantial numbers in the same way as the Western powers, or at least abstained and refused to vote against the West, as in the fifteenth session on the question of the admission of Communist China.

On the Congo question, a sharp cleavage developed among the African delegations. The members of the Casablanca grouping, in particular Guinea and Mali, on the one hand, pressed for strong, forceful measures by the UN to compel President Tshombé of Katanga Province to desist from demands for independence and to remain a part of a unified Congolese state. The members of the territorially closer Brazzaville grouping, on the other hand, were outspoken in opposition to the military operations of the UNOC (UN Operations in the Congo) forces and were often critical of UN activities in the area. For their part they were sympathetic to and supported the stand of Mr. Tshombé in favor of a loose confederation.

One could see in these postures, on the one hand, the fears of such leaders as Nkrumah and Touré that success on the part of Tshombé in rebelling against a central regime might give encouragement to resistance to their own totalitarian-like regimes and create a precedent for UN sanction of separatism. Members of the Brazzaville grouping, on the other hand, wished to forestall the rise of a potentially powerful, highly centralized regime in the heart of black Africa. They viewed Tshombé as a bulwark against a possible communist threat and as a stable element in the chaotic Congo political situation. Moreover, they disliked the spectacle of the UN intervening in what they considered to be a domestic situation. For what was done here could easily become a precedent for UN intervention in other internal disruptions or situations irrespective of the injunction in Article 2, paragraph 7, of the Charter against intervention by the World Body in "matters which are essentially within the domestic jurisdiction of any state." There was far more than a legal technicality at stake in the contrary positions taken by various African states on the Congo affair.[2] Nevertheless, despite this common attitude, the Brazzaville grouping, like the others, has failed to maintain a unified front on this problem during the fifteenth and sixteenth sessions.

On what might be generalized as "other questions," and even on matters that slip into the East-West struggle but are of distinct and direct vital concern to the African states per se, these countries have lined up with the West when they have found its position compatible with what they conceive to be their particular interests. Thus, in 1961, the African states were generally opposed to the Soviet Union's "troika" proposal for the Secretary-Generalship. Where their emotional desires for a peaceful world are brought into play they may find themselves in agreement with the Soviet bloc against the West, as happened at the sixteenth session on the draft resolution calling for an immediate nuclear test moratorium without international inspection pending conclusion of a general arms control agreement. On economic aid and development proposals looking toward larger expenditures or more liberal loan arrangements, the African states generally can be expected, out of what they conceive to be their own self-interests, to vote for larger, more costly programs than the Western powers are willing to accept. And many of them, faced as they are with the most difficult economic and financial outlooks, can be expected to cast their votes against heavier assessments or to resist making contributions for carrying out these programs.

III. Associations with Asian States—Influence of Membership in Afro-Asian Caucus

An important element in the activities of the African states at the United Nations is their participation in the larger Afro-Asian caucus. Although the Asian members are numerically fewer than the African, and although the principle of alphabetical rotation is followed each month in the choice of president, the pervasive influence within this caucus is unquestionably Asian. This development reflects several influences among which are the cumulative effects of the Bandung, the Afro-Asian, and the All-African Peoples Conferences, and the decisive support supplied by the Asian UN Members over the past

---

[2] For an incisive discussion of this problem see R. C. Good, "Four Tendencies at the United Nations," *Africa Report*, June 1961 (Vol. 6, No. 6); and "Congo Crisis: The Role of the New States," in *Neutralism*, published by the Washington Center of Foreign Policy Research, 1961.

decade to the emerging African group in their campaign for the admission
of new Members from their continent. This has resulted in a generally close
coordination between a substantial number of the African states, especially
those forming the Casablanca grouping, and the Asian "neutralists," who
often appear to be more pro-Soviet in their stance than genuinely neutral
in the full sense of the term.

In view of all the subtle differences in the outlooks and policies of the
various African and Asian states it is difficult to affix any hard and fast number to the Afro-Asian caucus members that are "pro-East," "pro-West," or
"neutralist." During the fifteenth and sixteenth sessions of the General
Assembly, voting alignments of Asian and African states on a number of
highly political issues seemed to imply that a majority of these states were
"pro-Eastern." But this interpretation can be deceptive. For not every time
African states and the communist powers voted alike were the Africans voting *for* the Soviets; quite often it was the Moscow-controlled bloc trying to
identify itself with Africans and Asians in order to insinuate the notion that
Moscow is their true friend and supporter.

The voting margins have been too tenuous to permit the projection of any
assured conclusions. On some of the most important contests at the fifteenth
and sixteenth sessions substantial numbers, including some at least of the
largest and potentially most effective leaders in the African scene, voted with
the Western powers. Again, on some items the voting result was as much
an identification of certain Western powers, especially the United States,
with African positions and interests as vice versa. Thus, one must be careful
in applying a "pro-West" label simply because of surface appearances of the
voting tallies.

No hard and fast pattern is discernible as yet among the lists of abstainers
on General Assembly votes. These vary with the issues presented and the
diplomacy that goes on behind the scenes and within the UN walls. Somalia,
Togo, and the Congo (Brazzaville) abstained on a high percentage of votes
at the fifteenth and sixteenth sessions. About all one can say is that African
states, like some others, are quick to take advantage of the protective camouflage which the international conference machinery can offer.

IV. The Issue of Self-Determination

On no question have Africans felt more strongly than on self-determination. From the time that a sense of national consciousness began to stir
among the African peoples, and leaders began to call for an ending of colonial ties, the concept of self-determination became the principal touchstone
of African politics. Although this was not always spelled out in precise
terms, the meaning was clear: sever the colonial rule, give the lands inde-

pendence, let the African peoples decide for themselves what policies should be applied within their lands, within Africa as a whole, and what role their country should occupy in international relations. Along with this went, in many cases, resentments born of the sense of class consciousness, racial discrimination, and inequalities of social and educational opportunity which Africans so often experienced.

There is little question that the struggle for self-determination, and the need for friends and supporters within the United Nations on matters affecting the destinies of Africa, contributed to the coalescing of the African and the Asian states during the 1950's. For Asians too were preoccupied with similar issues in their own part of the world.

In the settlement of the problems of the former Italian colonies after World War II, including especially the assignment of Somalia to Italian trusteeship, Africans felt that African self-determination was at stake and they saw non-Africans making the decisions. Likewise, within the Trusteeship Council and in the General Assembly non-African combinations determined what should be done with respect to the trusteeships and the non-self-governing territories in Africa. All of these incidents, plus the struggles of Tunisia and Morocco for independence, together with hatred of the *apartheid* policies being pursued in South Africa against the black man, fired emotions and fed the urge to obtain the right of self-determination.

Viewed in the large, the long struggle for self-determination in Africa, both north and south of the Sahara, came to eventual fruition outside rather than within the United Nations. In a very real sense the UN was instrumental in advancing the independence of Somalia, Togoland, the Cameroons, and Tanganyika by means of the stimulus, pressures, and assistance brought to bear through the trusteeship system. The UN certainly aided Libya in achieving its independence and establishing its statehood. It would be foolhardy to say that the debates and resolutions in the General Assembly on the Tunisian and Moroccan questions in 1950–1951 did not play some part in hastening ultimate French agreement to their independence. And at the time of Suez, the actions of the special emergency session of the General Assembly in calling by an overwhelming vote for a cease-fire and the withdrawal of British, French, and Israeli forces from Egyptian soil, together with the establishment of the UN Emergency Force to take over at Suez and then to police the Gaza Strip, certainly were not an insignificant factor in preserving the independence and the integrity of Egypt.

For the vast majority of the newly-independent states, nevertheless, actions taken by Britain, France, and Belgium outside the Organization through collaboration or at last agreement with the nationalist leaders of the various lands were the decisive factor in their attainment of independence. It is understandable, therefore, that while the African states have been eager to

become Members of the World Organization for the prestige, sense of equality, and economic and technical assistance which they may gain from it or
through it, their leaders and people adhere to the view that their independence has been achieved largely through their own efforts rather than through
the United Nations.

V. Current Concern for Status Quo and Territorial Integrity

With the attainment of independence, the African states have now
"crossed the divide" from the dynamics of "self-determination" into the area
of status—that is, the maintenance of independence and of frontiers—and
the protection of territorial integrity. Positions are now reversed. The concept of territorial integrity is a meeting place of the old quest for self-determination and the new concern for status quo. With this reversal comes a
fear lest the United Nations should serve as a means or instrumentality to
re-establish, in one form or another, the *"status quo ante."* And with this
one sees the anomaly of certain Western states pressing for self-determination in Algeria, the Congo, and New Guinea over Afro-Asian opposition.

For many of the African states the problem has become transformed from
the political issue of urging self-determination to the legal and political one
of insisting on territorial integrity. Such a concept has no meaning in itself
without the territorial definition supplied by the adoption of the existing
boundaries drawn in the past by the colonial powers, however artificial they
may be in terms of ethnic, economic, or geographic factors.

The magnitude of the dangers which may be involved in the further
application of the principle of "self-determination" to peoples within the
emerged states can be sensed in the facts that the Lunda, Chokwe, Bakongo,
and Azande tribes extend far beyond the borders of the Congo into Northern Rhodesia, Angola, the Congo (Brazzaville), the Central African Republic, and the Sudan, respectively; that the Somalis lay claim to one-third of
Ethiopia as well as to a substantial portion of Kenya; and that the Ewe cut
across the frontiers of Ghana, Togo, and Dahomey. It is not without moment that President Sylvanus Olympio of Togo, who launched his career
by serving as spokesman at the General Assembly for a Ewe national state,
should now look with favor on the retention of the present non-ethnical
boundaries of Togo.[3]

It is not surprising that African and Asian states supported and frequently
invoke the provisions of resolution 1514, passed at the fifteenth session of
the General Assembly, calling for respect for territorial integrity. Nor is it
unusual that they should resist efforts to make Ruanda-Urundi into two

[3] S. Olympio, "African Problems in the Cold War," *Foreign Affairs*, October 1961 (Vol. 40, No. 1),
p. 50–57.

separate states in accordance with the alleged desires of the populations rather than a unified state. It was in keeping with the same attitude that the majority of the Afro-Asian states opposed draft resolution A/L.368 presented at the sixteenth session by the Brazzaville group, and supported by the Netherlands, calling for the application of self-determination to the settlement of the problem of New Guinea. Speaking in opposition to this proposal the Indian delegate declared:

> you cannot split up the peoples of any country. If you do that then what is there left? . . . Are we going to push this principle of self-determination, however good it might be, to destroy the integrity of States and to affect the sovereignty of countries?

And the Indonesian delegate affirmed that "the recent history of the Congo offers ample proof that full self-determination based upon regional or ethnical considerations only creates confusion and suffering for the people concerned."[4]

Thus, the United Nations is faced with the seemingly paradoxical situation in which some African and Asian states that had formerly long and strenuously pressed for "self-determination" in North Africa now align themselves to block a proposal to that end offered by other African states. The piquancy and measure of the reversal are further revealed by the fact to which the representative of the Central African Republic made acidulous reference,[5] that the opposition to self-determination for New Guinea rested essentially on espousal of the Dutch colonial definition of the territories.[6] The position of the Brazzaville group has been almost equally clear; in 1961 it opposed a UN plebiscite in Algeria,[7] and through its leader, the representative of the Ivory Coast, it expressed support for the recognition of pre-existing colonial frontiers in Africa.[8]

---

[4] A/PV.1065, November 27, 1961.

[5] "One of the principal arguments advanced in support of that thesis by Mr. Subandrio . . . is that when a colonial territory accedes to independence, its sovereignty should be exercised within the limits of the former colonial sovereignty. This is a principle which is doubtless quite just in most cases, but certain qualifications must be introduced when it is a question of territories whose peoples are not united by racial or cultural links or by common beliefs." A/PV.1065.

[6] "The right of self-determination applies, of course, to the entire population *of a colony as a unit and to the entire territory of a colony as a unit* [italics added] . . . . The right of self-determination is not something to be applied to racial, cultural, or ethnic groups *within a colony.*" A/PV.1065, November 27, 1961, Subandrio, representative of Indonesia.

[7] "In our opinion, the problem of self-determination raises several awkward problems . . . We consider that we could never agree to the right of self-determination being exercised otherwise than for the whole body of the Algerian people and for the whole of the Algerian territory." A/PV.956, December 19, 1960, D'Arboussier, representative of Senegal.

[8] "At the moment of accession towards independence, in order to avoid internecine wars which might jeopardize the independence just acquired with such difficulty it was agreed to accept the territorial limits obtaining at that time." A/PV.1043, October 27, 1961. The political relations between the Congo (Brazzaville) and the Congo (Leopoldville), in general, and with respect to the provinces of Katanga and Leopoldville, in particular, cannot be ignored in this connection.

Sensitive to press criticism of the ambivalent stand taken by some on the Congo situation, the Foreign Minister of Nigeria at one point observed:

Where, they said, is the principle of self-determination as regards Katanga? I said the following: how would you as an American like it if the State of New York or the State of California were to be cut off from the United States because the people wanted self-determination?[9]

Thus, following the example of the Latin American states in the nineteenth century, the African states, having won the struggle against colonialism, are now insisting upon respect of pre-existing colonial boundaries.[10] Ethiopia has long contended for the validity of the boundary line drawn between itself and the territory·of Somalia by the treaty with Italy in 1908. Recently the representative of Liberia, the frontiers of which had been determined by agreements with colonial powers, cautioned others with these words:

We know that brothers and sisters were separated mutually by boundaries imposed to meet the requirements of the colonial powers. Much as we deplore those arbitrary acts, those boundaries have become fixed after a period of time and form all boundaries of the independent African States. What chaos, what confusion, what hatred could be engendered by each of the new African countries against each other were those boundaries to be changed or readjusted . . . My advice to my fellow African States, especially those that live in African States, is to let sleeping dogs lie.[11]

And in similar vein the Foreign Minister of Nigeria remarked at the sixteenth session:

I am not happy to listen in this Assembly and find one African State raising a question of a boundary dispute with another State here when in fact we can treat this as a domestic affair and deal with the matter at home. I am appealing to all concerned: African States, do not make speeches at this rostrum about boundary questions. That is why my country, in its foreign policy says, "Leave these territories as they are."[12]

Thus it appears that the General Assembly is not likely to become the forum in which decisions will be taken on controversies relating to boundaries in Africa if the African states can prevent it.

[9] A/PV.1031, October 10, 1961. See also opposition of the Sudan, itself a former beneficiary of self-determination. A/PV.1065, November 27, 1961, Ambassador Adeel on West Irian question.

[10] See Rupert Emerson, *From Empire to Nation* (Cambridge: Harvard University Press, 1960), Chapters VI and XVI.

[11] It would seem that the basic issue involved in the recent admission of Mauritania was less the threat to the territorial integrity of Morocco, as exploited by it in the discussions, than the threat to African boundary treaties generally if the colonial arrangements establishing the frontiers of Mauritania were to be drawn into question by the General Assembly through refusal to admit Mauritania to membership.

[12] A/PV.1031, October 10, 1961.

The same deep-seated concern for preserving their territorial integrity and independence can be said to underlie the suspicion with which some African states have viewed the activities of the Secretariat in the Congo and elsewhere. These actions have stirred fears lest the United Nations should intrude upon their independence or integrity, or should in effect re-establish a form of trusteeship in lands which have but recently emerged from this status. Thus, even before the Congo crisis, the proposal of the Secretary-General to establish a UN "presence" in Africa in the form of personal ambassadors, as previously attempted in the Middle East and Southeast Asia, evoked serious misgivings in African quarters.

The sudden interposition of the Secretary-General in the final phase of the boundary discussions between Ethiopia and Somalia in 1958 for the announced purpose of resolving the issues by his personal intervention was felt to be a factor contributing to the breakdown of negotiations and the failure to obtain a solution of this issue. Similarly, truce talks with the government of Katanga have produced periods of sudden opposition and obstructionism. There is a pervasive fear among African states lest the Secretariat be inspired to action along the lines of the late Secretary-General's political testament contained in the introduction to his last annual report.[13] If it is true that to a degree the General Assembly has assumed parliamentary powers, then the assertion of political and executive functions by the Secretary-General would exacerbate the fears already entertained with regard to the Assembly. Yet, such a course claimed the support of the late Secretary-General.[14]

The African states were, consequently, in the main laconic in their defense of the Secretary-General when at the fifteenth session he came under attack from the Soviet bloc for allegedly overreaching his powers. This did not preclude, however, their standing firm against Soviet machinations to replace the Secretary-General with a triumvirate that could be blocked at any moment by a veto from within the office by the Soviets or the West or a "neutralist." On the contrary, they used their persuasion and influence to elect an acting Secretary-General who albeit was from an Asian neutralist country. Although U Thant was known for active diplomacy on behalf of his country, he had not prior to his election publicly espoused the late Secretary-General's theory of executive-political leadership.

---

[13] See *International Organization*, Autumn 1961 (Vol. 15, No. 4), p. 549–563.

[14] In his view, the Secretary-General was "one in whom there would be combined both the political and executive functions of a President with the internal administrative functions that were previously accorded to a Secretary-General. Obviously, this is a reflection, in some measure, of the American political system, which places authority in a chief executive officer who is not simply subordinated to the legislative organs but who is constitutionally responsible alone for the execution of legislation and in some respects for carrying out the authority derived from the constitutional instrument directly." Dag Hammarskjöld, *The International Civil Servant in Law and in Fact* (Oxford: Oxford University Press, 1961), p. 11.

VI. Conclusion

The present attitude of many African states is scarcely one of unbounded confidence in United Nations operations. There is some hope, however, that the UN can be beneficial to these states, in helping them preserve their territorial integrity and in extending to them increased economic and technical assistance. The fact that the African states are able to work together with the Asian states on many questions has given them a measure of assurance that in the General Assembly at least their views can be registered with effect and that proposals which they deem inimical to their interests can be blocked. Conceivably, the transformation of some political questions into juridical ones, or at least their acquisition of a more highly juridical coloration than before, may well lead to disposition to refer some legal disputes relating to such matters as boundary lines to adjudication by the International Court of Justice. To the extent that this should occur in place of public debate and bloc voting in the General Assembly it would amount to a departure from reliance upon the Afro-Asian caucus with its numerous cross-currents and uncertainties.

For many problems regional institutions and solutions may serve a useful purpose in the African scene. The convening of no less than 25 regional conferences since 1957, and the recent organizational proposals of Casablanca, Monrovia, Dakar, and Lagos lend support to this hypothesis. A comment by President Youlou of the Congo (Brazzaville) exemplifies a feeling that is widely prevalent: "We cannot allow the fate of our brothers on the other side of the Congo to be decided quite arbitrarily by those who do not know their country and their spirit . . . Africa is our affair, our problems cannot, I repeat, be solved by any but ourselves, the great African family."

It is quite conceivable that African states which resent the discussion of African problems at the UN could accept to do so *en famille,* by "palaver" as it were, in regional meetings removed from the UN. Although the movement toward regionalism has already produced rival systems, the desire to find accord through regional channels cannot be gainsaid.

The success of the moderate elements at the Monrovia and Dakar gatherings in May and June of 1961, and the results achieved at Lagos in January 1962, give solid reason for encouragement. Fortunately the Lagos grouping constitutes the largest, and at the moment, the most active, regional organization.[15] For the near future regionalism can perhaps afford a theater in which relations between the West and African states might be explored without the handicaps of protective coloration or parliamentary compromise that must almost inevitably appear when matters are being debated or voted

[15] See Rupert Emerson, "Pan-Africanism," in this issue, p. 275–290; and Erasmus H. Kloman, Jr., "African Unification Movements," *ibid.,* p. 387–404.

upon within the United Nations. At the same time the United Nations can continue as a forum in which the African personality can be brought to bear upon world problems, whether in a unified or divided voice. It can provide an instrumentality for helping to keep or to restore peace, for mobilizing political pressures to speed the process of independence for the remaining colonial lands. And, of course, it is in the eyes of all Africans an indispensable channel for the funneling of economic, financial, and technical assistance for the realization of their aspirations of economic growth and cultural advancement.

AFRICAN UNIFICATION MOVEMENTS

Erasmus H. Kloman, Jr.

The numerous unification efforts now under way in Africa represent one of the most significant developments in the brief post-independence era of that continent. Freedom has brought with it increased recognition in many African quarters of the interdependence of the African states and the need for unified approaches to common problems. The new countries together with the handful of older independent African states have nearly all become involved in one or more of the intensified drives toward some form of integration. Paradoxically, the issue of how to achieve unity is becoming one of the principal divisions between African states.

In view of the centuries it has taken the western European nations to progress just to the point where the European movement stands today, it is scarcely remarkable that as yet unification efforts in Africa have not evolved into a single rational and steady movement. On the contrary, the directness of the head-on approach which sovereign African states have taken to promote closer cooperation or unity with each other is one of the outstanding and possibly more promising features on the contemporary African political scene.

Nationalism in the independent states of Africa is a very recent development and is far less deeply rooted than the history-laden nationalism which has plagued the European movement. Even so, many of the nationalist-inspired rivalries between African states are not easily bridged. Nationalism in the new African states had its origins in the colonial era. The nineteenth century partitioning of Africa by the European powers resulted inevitably in the isolation of the colonies from each other. Having been oriented for so long toward metropolitan capitals with antipathetic colonial policies and differing cultural systems, the African states have had some difficulty in replacing these past colonial associations with new intra-African relationships. The colonial administrations in Africa deserve full credit for the benefits they brought and indeed for the provision of the only available means of transition from tribal society to modern statehood. At the same time it must be acknowledged that the European powers were late in recognizing the intrinsic value of unity in Africa and have only recently begun

ERASMUS H. KLOMAN, JR. is in the Office of the Chairman, American Metal Climax, Inc. in New York. This study was made while he was serving as Assistant to the Director of the Foreign Policy Research Institute at the University of Pennsylvania. Mr. Kloman had previously served in the Department of State where, from 1950 to 1953, he was Special Assistant to the Assistant Secretary of State for Public Affairs.

to encourage any of the more far-reaching unification efforts which seek to bridge the gaps between former colonial empires.

Advocates of Pan-Africanism, one of the oldest of the continent's unification movements, have often proposed as a goal a "United States of Africa." They have sought to apply to Africa some version of the principle of federal union which has achieved such success in the United States. But Africa today faces far different and, in some ways, more complex problems than those which confronted the thirteen colonies. Africa is less homogeneous, less compact, and far less prepared politically, economically, and socially for federal union. Nor is Africa, as was the United States in its infancy, able to escape pressures created by outside forces seeking to play power politics.

Most African leaders are not really interested in the Cold War struggle between East and West and would prefer to remain apart from it so as to concentrate on finding solutions to Africa's pressing internal problems. But the nature of the Cold War, or more particularly the communist strategy for waging it, is such that no important area of the world can avoid being touched by the struggle. An area such as Africa which combines strategic and economic importance with a vast potential for unrest and instability can only be a prime target for communist bloc penetration and subversion.

The ideological conflict on which the Cold War struggle is based is already reflected to a significant degree in the conflict between differing African approaches to unification. Few African leaders are willing to renounce all aspects of Marxist socialism as an unmitigated evil. Many are willing to borrow from the experience of communist countries which have dealt with problems similar to those confronting Africa; some are willing to go much further than others in this borrowing process.

All African leaders proclaim their neutralism or, as they prefer to call it, "nonalignment" in the Cold War. But, in the international relationships of the African states, a wide variety of interpretations is discernible in their foreign policies and international connections. While the cultural ties and sympathies of some countries remain primarily with the former colonial powers and the nations of the West, a few African regimes have moved far in the direction of closer ties with the communist world. The leaders of these regimes believe that the most effective means of increasing their political leverage and obtaining outside economic aid is a hard-hitting neutralist game in which East and West are played off against each other.

While important differences undoubtedly distinguish the political leanings among various African leaders and factions, including those which separate Nkrumah from the more moderate elements, these differences should not be allowed to obscure the goals which African nationalists share in common. They all declare themselves dedicated to improving the standards of living of the African peoples, to increasing Africa's influence in world affairs, to maintaining African neutralism in the Cold War struggle, to winning the independence of the remaining African dependencies, and to promoting unity among all the African nations. These goals may seem to be of such a general nature and so far from fulfillment as to have little bearing on contemporary African affairs. But the similarities in objectives provide an important common bond between all African nationalist movements. The advocates of Pan-Africanism know that their appeals have a ready audience among the millions of Africans throughout the continent who are making the sometimes exhilarating but usually painful transition from primitive to civilized society. Thus Nkrumah, though he may be mistrusted by many leaders and elites outside Ghana, has struck a responsive chord among the masses in many other parts of the continent.

One stimulus toward unity is represented by the common continent-wide interests from which Pan-Africanism draws its strength. A second stimulus, the attraction of regionalism, also exerts a strong influence, playing an increasingly important role in shaping the make-up of African groupings. In a mood similar to that which is drawing the nations of Europe closer together, neighboring nations in Africa seek ways to combine their physical and human resources and to minimize the sometimes harmful effects of boundaries arbitrarily imposed in the colonial partitioning of Africa.

The Casablanca powers, as we shall note more fully below, are concentrated in North Africa with a smaller but powerful appendage in West Africa. A second grouping, the Monrovia powers, cover the rest of West Africa and middle Africa. Now a third grouping is evolving in East, Central, and southern Africa. An intriguing but highly debatable question is whether regionalism or ideology is exercising the greater pull in determining the make-up and character of African groupings.

The pace of change far exceeds the expectation of those who knew Africa in the earlier era of colonialism. The consolidation movements now under way are both an instrument and a symptom of change. In order to assess the strengths and weaknesses of these various movements, the following analysis seeks to examine briefly their origins, their orientations, and their interrelationships.

Ghana-Guinea-Mali Union (Union of African States)

When, in 1958, Guinea elected to stay out of the French Community, it had made a breach in that institution which has never been sealed. France's injured pride, abetted by the prodding of President Houphouet-Boigny of the Ivory Coast, prompted the ill-conceived French retaliatory withdrawal from Guinea. Ghana's Nkrumah was quick in offering to form an association with a fellow revolutionary, President Sékou Touré of Guinea. In very short order the two leaders announced a constitutional union of their two countries, encompassing common economic policies, a £10 million loan by Ghana to Guinea, and even some combination of parliamentary institutions.

When Mali (formerly Soudan) subsequently broke off from an abortive federation with Senegal in 1960, it joined Ghana and Guinea in what is officially called the Union of African States. The three countries met in Bamako in July 1961, and issued a charter of union which called for a mutual defense agreement and cooperation in diplomatic, economic, cultural, and research activities. No common institutions were authorized in the charter but the conferences of the three heads of state were regarded as the union's supreme body.

Thus far this much-vaunted union has appeared to be of uncertain substance. Guinea has even exhibited a reluctance to take full advantage of its loan from Ghana. Talk of a common currency has proved to be no more than talk, and there have been no joint parliamentary sessions. Ghana, which first took the initiative in promoting this arrangement, appears to be the only member of the union with unreserved enthusiasm for its perpetuation.

Upper Volta finds itself a territorial interposition between the three members of this union. A question of considerable moment in the political evolution of West Africa hinges, therefore, on Upper Volta's future course. Nkrumah has busied himself for some time with overtures toward this northern neighbor and already the two countries have entered into agreements on broadening exchanges and eliminating border controls. Although Upper Volta has not been able to conclude as favorable economic relationships with the Ivory Coast as had been hoped, its ties with the French-speaking countries are sufficiently strong to make Nkrumah's prospects for attaching Upper Volta to the Ghana-Guinea-Mali union appear slight. Should Nkrumah succeed, however, the entire power picture in West Africa would alter radically. Ghana, instead of being encircled by the French-speaking states of Ivory Coast, Upper Volta, and Togo, would dominate a new coalition which would encircle the Ivory Coast, Liberia, and Sierra Leone. As long as Upper Volta remains in the grouping of ex-French states centered on the Ivory Coast, the Ghana-Guinea-Mali union is deprived of any prospect of complete fulfillment. Nkrumah's wooing of President Yameogo of Upper Volta is poaching on the territory of the French-speaking African community. That community, however, is simultaneously encroaching on Nkrumah's territory by seeking to lure back into its fold both Guinea and Mali.

The Casablanca Powers

The Casablanca powers first met as a group in the capital of Morocco in early January 1961. Governments represented included the North African Arab states of Egypt, Morocco, and Libya together with the Algerian exile National Liberation Front (FLN) and the Ghana-Guinea-Mali trio. (Libya has since removed herself from this group to join the Monrovia powers.)

The ostensible reason for calling the Casablanca Conference was to coordinate African policies on the Congo. In reality, however, the most compelling consideration which led King Mohammed V of Morocco to convene the meeting was a sense of isolation following Morocco's defeat on the issue of its claim to hegemony over Mauritania at the General Assembly of the UN in December 1960. The other ex-French states were not invited to Casablanca because of their position favoring Mauritanian independence. Several other pro-Western states were invited but declined to attend. The Moroccan monarchy found itself in the somewhat anomalous position of embracing the most radical elements of African politics in a liaison which several weeks earlier would have seemed highly implausible.

The conference was hurriedly called as a counterpoise to the productive meeting of the twelve ex-French states at Brazzaville in December 1960. The Casablanca powers hoped to grab the ball of African unity before a rival faction could pick it up and run with it unopposed.

The meeting in Casablanca did not succeed in disguising the fact that those gathered there were beset by numerous internal differences. The competition between the expansionist ambitions of Nasser and Nkrumah was (and remains) an extremely divisive issue. Other questions dividing various nations of the Casablanca group include Mauritanian independence and conflicting claims to Saharan oil, as well as differing approaches toward Arab and North African unity. Almost the only common bond shared by the strange bedfellows whom misery brought together in the Casablanca grouping is that of "anti-colonialism," particularly evident in antipathy towards French North African policy. The Casablanca powers have earned the reputation of being the trouble-makers on the contemporary African political scene, but, fortunately for the West, they make trouble for each other in their uneasy union as well as for other states in Africa. The Casablanca grouping, in effect, represents the limits of progress which either Nkrumah or Nasser has made in fulfilling his competing Pan-African dreams of unity via formal association of nations.

All-African People's Conferences

Three All-African People's Conferences have been held: at Accra in 1958, at Tunis in 1960, and at Cairo in 1961. Nowhere has the divisive effect of the personal rivalry between Nkrumah and Nasser been more in evidence than in this series of conferences. In fact, the rivalry between these two leaders has threatened to vitiate the work of a network of political activists engaged in promoting the concept of African solidarity, notably in the Cairo and Accra Conference secretariats but also in centers scattered throughout the northern half of the African continent.

These conferences, as the name implies, are composed of representatives of private and unofficial organizations. Government representatives attend only as observers. A substantial portion of observers at each conference have been representatives of various communist bloc countries. The conferences and their permanent machinery serve as one of the principal channels for the introduction of communist funds into Africa.

When the All-African Conferences were initiated, the Soviets held out high hopes that they would provide a forum for uninhibited communist propaganda and agitation. But Nasser, who has consistently refused to legalize the Communist Party in the United Arab Republic, has disappointed Soviet hopes for an Egyptian fiefdom, demonstrating that he is not in anyone's pocket. A basic principle of Soviet strategy, however, is to probe every avenue of opportunity. If Nasser was not a willing tool, other African nationalists might prove more susceptible to Soviet blandishments. The communists are now working busily to infiltrate the African solidarity movements in an increasing number of African countries and particularly in Ghana, Guinea, Mali, Somalia, and the Congo (Leopoldville).

The third conference, from the viewpoint of its participants, was regarded as a letdown from previous meetings. Although numerous Soviet and Eastern bloc observers were on hand, the Soviet-Egyptian rift must have seemed a heavy pall on conference proceedings. The conference drew fewer African officials as observers than either of the preceding meetings in the series—an indication that interest was waning. Some 200 delegates representing a wide range of nonofficial organizations in independent and dependent territories took part in the meetings. But after passing five major resolutions similar to those adopted at many another gathering of anti-colonial nationalists, the conference disbanded without making any significant lasting impression on the African political scene.

Conferences of Independent African States

The First Conference of Independent African States was held in Accra in April 1958, while the Second Conference took place in Addis Ababa in June 1960. Five of the members of the Casablanca grouping—the United Arab Republic, Libya, Morocco, Ghana, and Guinea (an observer)—attended the Accra conference. Other countries represented at each of these two meetings included Ethiopia, Liberia, Sudan, and Tunisia. Attendance at the second conference was augmented by observers from Angola, Kenya, South Africa, South West Africa, Tanganyika, Uganda, Northern and Southern Rhodesia, Ruanda-Urundi, Sierra Leone, and Cameroun—the only French territory represented. Conferences in this series are scheduled for every two years, and the 1962 meeting will be held early in April in Tunis.

The intellectual origin of this series of meetings was the 1945 Pan-African Nationalist Conference held in Manchester, England, whose moving spirits included Nkrumah, Kenyatta, and the West Indian Negro, George Padmore. The latter subsequently became adviser on African affairs to Prime Minister Nkrumah. Before his death in 1959, Padmore exercised a very strong influence on Nkrumah and perhaps more than any other single individual helped to transform Pan-Africanism from an idea into a political movement.

Other forebearers of this African conference series were the Bandung Conference in 1955 and the Cairo Conference in 1957 of the Afro-Asian neutralist countries. The Accra Conference in 1958 reaffirmed the Bandung declaration of 1955 and passed other resolutions expressing "grave alarm" at Great Power politics and calling for a greater role for the neutralists in world affairs.

In order to assert their collective influence, at least in Africa, the independent African states have also held two special conferences on specific African problems. In August 1959, a conference on the Algerian problem was held in Monrovia. One year later a second conference took place in Leopoldville on the Congo crisis. Out of this latter meeting emerged the proposal, advanced by the Ghanaian delegation, to establish an African High Command. This military force was to be composed of troops assigned by independent African states and was to be charged with responsibility for safeguarding peace on the African continent. The proposal has not moved beyond the stage of discussion in committee although it has gained support from the Casablanca powers. Nkrumah has subsequently sought to promote the concept on numerous occasions without notable success in convincing non-Casablanca group leaders.

All-African Trade Union Federation (AATUF)

Still another facet of the Casablanca orientation in contemporary African affairs is the movement for establishment of the All-African Trade Union Federation. The motives of African union leaders in seeking to form an all-African labor federation independent of international labor organizations parallel the political drive toward Pan-Africanism. It may not seem surprising therefore that Ghana has been so prominent among the states seeking to dominate the movement toward unification of African labor organization.

After prolonged pulling and hauling among African labor leaders, a meeting intended to launch the controversial AATUF was finally held in late May 1961 in Casablanca where representatives of 45 African trade union organizations from some 30 African countries assembled. The rigged nature of the gathering became apparent as soon as the invitations for it were dispatched. Several representative African labor organizations were pointedly not invited. Those unions which accepted invitations were accredited by a preparatory committee weighted in favor of the Nkrumahist Casablanca wing. Heavy-handed discrimination in designating the voting power of various delegations, however, could not disguise the deep difference of opinion on the key issue before the conference, i.e. the Casablanca bloc's insistence on disaffiliation of African labor unions from existing international labor organizations in order to make way for the new AATUF.

Strong opposition to disaffiliation came from the delegations representing unions of Kenya, Tunisia, and Nigeria and most of the other twenty-odd unions affiliated with the International Confederation of Free Trade Unions (ICFTU)—the pro-Western international in which AFL-CIO plays an important role. The Ghana and Guinea delegations resorted to blatantly coercive tactics in steam-rollering through a vote for disaffiliation of all African unions within ten months after the signing of the proposed AATUF charter.

The communist-dominated World Federation of Trade Unions (WFTU) had long since prepared itself to back the Ghana-Guinea line at Casablanca by severing direct affiliations with all but one African labor union, the WFTU organization in Cameroun. The vote on disaffiliation was taken on the last day of the conference after a large percentage of the delegates had decided to boycott the meetings in order to demonstrate their opposition to the preparatory committee's tactics.

The Casablanca powers had manipulated a short-lived victory at Casablanca. John Tettegah, head of Ghana's Trades Union Congress, was named Secretary-General of the AATUF. But Tettegah's domination of the movement and the entire Casablanca orientation of the AATUF made it highly suspect in the eyes of those who had suffered defeat at the May conference.

African Trade Union Confederation (ATUC)

The Casablanca powers were not to be unchallenged for long in their play for control of African unionism. More moderate elements in the labor movement had been laying plans for establishing a competing organization even before the Casablanca meeting was held. In January 1962, this rival group convened in the Senegalese capital of Dakar. Those attending represented approximately 50 unions from 30 nations. They agreed to form a loose organization called the African Trade Union Confederation.

The main way in which the ATUC differs from the AATUF is that the former does not forbid the affiliation of African unions with international labor organizations. Thus, the effort to cut off the African labor unions from ties with Free World labor movements was, at least for the time being, foiled. Prior to Dakar, none of the unions in the AATUF had complied with the Casablanca Conference demand for disaffiliation.

The labor union movement usually plays an exceptionally influential role in the political affairs of African countries. No other segment of society is organized, and labor unions represent almost the only grass-roots organization aside from the somewhat primitive political party structure. Thus, the decision taken at Dakar to permit continued affiliation has an importance not only for the labor unions but for the political development of Africa as well. The Casablanca powers suffered a serious setback at Dakar.

The Brazzaville Powers (African-Malagasy Organization for Economic Cooperation)

As the Ghana-Guinea-Mali union forms a certain core of the Casablanca power group, so the Brazzaville powers represent a core of the Monrovia grouping. In December 1960, twelve of the newly independent French speaking African countries met in Brazzaville to form a loose community of states formerly tied to France. The twelve were Cameroun, Central African Republic, Chad, Congo Republic (Brazzaville), Dahomey, Gabon, Ivory Coast, Malagasy Republic, Mauritania, Niger, Senegal, and Upper Volta. In subsequent meetings in Dakar and Yaoundé in the early months of 1961 these twelve nations established the *Organisation Africaine et Malgache de Coopération Economique* (OAMCE). Guinea and Mali have been conspicuously absent from all of the Brazzaville group meetings despite serious efforts which continue to be made to bring these two strays back into the fold. Togo also remains outside of the Brazzaville group although it is one of the Monrovia grouping.

Among the specific objectives of the OAMCE are the establishment of a joint development program, a development bank, the formulation of common investment codes, and the coordination of relations with the European Common Market. The Brazzaville powers have already combined their individual air services in a common airline, Air Afrique.

The leadership of the Brazzaville group is contested, though somewhat dispassionately in comparison with other intra-African political jockeying, among various leaders of the French Community. President Tsiranana of Malagasy is President of the OAMCE, but probably the greatest political power rests in the hands of President Houphouet-Boigny of the Ivory Coast. Houphouet-Boigny not only retains a considerable influence in political cir-

cles in France but also occupies a strategic position as head of the largest
and strongest political party in ex-French West Africa, the *Rassemblement
Démocratique Africain* (RDA). He has a strong attachment to France, to
Western values, and to the free enterprise system. Houphouet-Boigny's
fundamental problem is one of maintaining the basic positions which he per-
sonally favors in the face of powerful African nationalist forces challenging
him from the left.

The Brazzaville powers are motivated primarily by a sense of belonging
to a French-speaking community. Their cultural and spiritual fountainhead
is Paris. They have benefited and continue to benefit far more than the
ex-British countries from their economic association with their former
mother country. The OAMCE, in confining itself to the ex-French territories, is an exclusivist grouping, although each of the member states realizes
the importance of broadening contacts and trade with non-French African
countries.

Conseil de l'Entente

Houphouet-Boigny's strong position in French-speaking Africa is also
reinforced by his commanding position in the *Conseil de l'Entente* consist-
ing of the four contiguous states of the Ivory Coast, Niger, Upper Volta, and
Dahomey. Formed in May 1959, the *Conseil de l'Entente* comprises a customs union as well as a "Solidarity Fund" for financial assistance to each of
the member states. Monies are contributed to this fund by each of the four
countries on the basis of a formula reflecting capacity to pay and withdrawn
in a roughly inverse ratio according to need. The Ivory Coast is by far the
largest contributor. The *Conseil de l'Entente* has also provided for the coordination of the development plans of the four states and of their policies
in the fields of taxation, public administration, labor legislation, public
works, transportation, and communications.

The *Conseil de l'Entente* came into being as the result of a coup executed
by Houphouet-Boigny in luring Upper Volta and Dahomey away from a
short-lived association with the abortive Mali Federation. This coup helped
to give him a stronger power position than the political leadership of Senegal which had traditionally dominated French West African affairs. The
future of the *Conseil* will depend on the relationship it is to have with the
OAMCE and the still larger Monrovia grouping.

The Monrovia Powers

The grouping of twenty states which have come to be called the Monrovia
powers met in the Liberian capital in May 1961. Most of the countries attending were represented by heads of state: the Brazzaville nations of

Cameroun, Chad, Congo Republic (Brazzaville), Dahomey, the Ivory Coast, Malagasy Republic, Mauritania, Niger, Senegal, and Upper Volta—as well as Liberia, Nigeria, Sierra Leone, Somalia, and Togo. In addition, high-level delegations represented Tunisia (whose President could not attend because of his state visits to the United States, the United Kingdom, and Canada), the Central African Republic and Gabon (whose Presidents were ill), Ethiopia, and Libya.

The Monrovia Conference was an important landmark in the labyrinthian pattern of African bloc politics. It was the largest assemblage of top leaders of independent African states yet to convene. The tone of discussions and the resolutions passed at the conference reflected a wide area of agreement on questions pertaining to Africa's political and economic future. Tafawa Balewa, Prime Minister of Nigeria, emerged as a dominating personality. His moderation which prevailed throughout was in large measure responsible for agreement on a gradual and functional approach toward unification in place of an extreme Pan-Africanist approach. Indeed, the Monrovia Conference was a direct challege to Nkrumah. The London *Times* correspondent covering the meeting observed that it marked "the beginning of the end of Ghana's leadership in Africa."

The Lagos Meeting of African Heads of State

The Monrovia conferees empowered a standing committee to make preparations for an African summit which was held at Lagos in late January 1961. Great expectations had been aroused as the time for the Lagos meeting approached, and hope was held out until the last that this meeting might be attended by representatives of the Casablanca powers so that the gap between them and the Monrovia powers might be at least narrowed.

Exactly the opposite occurred. The Casablanca states announced their decision not to attend just before the preliminary meetings of the Lagos Conference got under way. The announcement, which came from Accra, charged that the decision of the Lagos conferees not to invite representatives of the Algerian FLN threatened to undermine the Algerian independence movement. The Casablanca powers, therefore, could not attend. Guinea and Mali were reported to have favored participation, but were firmly reined in by Ghana.

The Casablanca powers had to decide whether they could thwart the moderate leadership of the Lagos meeting more effectively by boycotting or by attending and subverting from within. The fact that the rift has been kept out in the open may be in the long-run interests of the moderate influence which remains dominant among the Monrovia grouping.

Countries present at Lagos were the same as at Monrovia except that Libya and Tunisia dropped out on the issue of Algerian representation while the Congo (Leopoldville) and Tanganyika were added to the ranks. The conference, which was preceded by a foreign ministers' meeting, was attended by seventeen heads of state or government out of the twenty nations represented.

The meeting authorized formation of working committees at cabinet level to coordinate regional activities in the areas of economic development, trade, education, health, agriculture, transport, and communications. It approved in principle a charter for an inter-African and Malagasy states organization which, if implemented, would far transcend any previous effort to give content to the goal of African unity. The charter provided for two high-level forums—an assembly of heads of states and a council of ministers—together with a permanent secretariat to administer the organization's committees and commissions. The final plan for all of this organizational structure was to be worked out by a meeting of foreign ministers later this year.

The Lagos conferees displayed a strong determination to put into effect the decisions they had taken, if for no other reason than because failure to do so would leave the field open to the Casablanca powers. Should the Lagos resolutions be fulfilled, the meeting will have been perhaps the most important single step on the road toward African unity since independence. If the decisions are not implemented, Lagos will mark a turning point at which the momentum gathered hitherto by the Monrovia powers will be seen to be slackening to the detriment of the cause of unity via the gradual and functional approach.

East African Common Services Organization (formerly East Africa High Commission)

West Africa remains sharply divided, as of the present writing, between conflicting orientations. Perhaps a somewhat more hopeful prospect for unity may be found in current developments in East Africa.

The 1961 agreement to establish the East African Common Services Organization was one of the more promising signs on the African political front. Largely on the initiative of Prime Minister Nyerere, representatives of the governments of Tanganyika, Kenya, and Uganda, together with an observer from Zanzibar, met at the British Colonial Office in London in June 1961 to formulate plans for cooperation during the interval when Tanganyika was to achieve independence and the other two were still working toward it. Basically, the new organization represents a continuation of the functions formerly carried out by the East Africa High Commission established in 1948. That Commission, which consisted of the Governors of the three territories, together with a representative of Zanzibar, provided a joint administration of communications, transport, customs, currency, and various technical services.

The new East African Common Services Organization came into effect in December 1961, when Tanganyika achieved independence. Specifically, it coordinates communication, finance, commerce, and social services in the three East African countries. Perhaps the most significant aspect of the new institution is the fact that responsibility for its administration rests with three African elected ministers—the Prime Minister of Tanganyika, and the principal elected ministers of each of the other two territories.

The British government has shown great discretion by allowing the initiative for the africanization of an institution which it created to appear to come from Africans. The institution can only be strengthened by the change. Nyerere, for his part, has again given evidence of his moderation and statesmanship by agreeing to share equal partnership with two territories that are still working toward independence.

Functional cooperation through the East African Common Services Organization could pave the way for a federal political grouping in East Africa. The federal approach, it is widely hoped, would help to bring harmony not only in the relations between the member states but also for dealing with a number of thorny issues which otherwise have little chance of being resolved—such as the opposition of the Baganda and other feudalists to formation of a national state of Uganda, the Arab Irredentism on the Kenya coast, and the Masai tribal objections to being divided by the Kenya-Tanganyika border.

An East African federation, if it should come into being, would not be a panacea for all of East Africa's ills. A certain rivalry between the member states is natural and inevitable. This could manifest itself in a political struggle between Kenyatta of Kenya and Nyerere of Tanganyika for leadership, though Nyerere has offered the presidency of any federation that emerges to Kenyatta. Since his release Kenyatta has disappointed British hopes that he might unite the country behind him in an orderly movement toward independence. An unexpected aloofness and a certain ambiguity seem to have reduced Kenyatta's once powerful appeal. A failure to achieve some national unity in Kenya would bode ill for the prospects of East African unity.

Nevertheless, some encouragement may be derived from Nyerere's decision to stake his and Tanganyika's lot with that of their fellow East African nations even though they lag somewhat behind in progress towards independence. Nyerere has eschewed the extreme nationalist approach which would have favored a sovereign Tanganyika going it alone. By so doing he may well have improved the prospects for his own and his country's leadership in East African affairs.

The prospect for the continuation of an East African economic association under African control carries the highest significance for Northern Rhodesia and Nyasaland. Both territories might become candidates for membership in such a regional grouping. Even Southern Rhodesia could become eligible in the event that white minority rule should ultimately give way to rule by a black majority. Southern Rhodesia could form a bridge linking the East African grouping to Bechuanaland and, conceivably, to an independent South West Africa. All these countries share the heritage of British colonialism. English is the national language in each of them. Finally, the island of Zanzibar and the two states which will emerge from Ruanda-Urundi, being contiguous with Uganda and Tanganyika, would seem to fit logically into an East African grouping. Somalia is another possible addition.

Pan-African Freedom Movement of East, Central, and South Africa (PAFMECSA)

The formal basis for regional cooperation between nationalist movements in East and Central Africa emerged from a 1958 meeting at Mwanza on the shores of Lake Victoria. Nationalist leaders from Kenya, Uganda, Tanganyika, Nyasaland, and Zanzibar met together to form what came to be known as PAFMECA. This East African variant of the Pan-African movement, although it had roots in an earlier period, was given concrete expression considerably later than its counterpart in West Africa.

The West African countries, being less under the dominion of white settler minorities, were more advanced politically. The Pan-African movement thus had its first foothold in the British and French countries of West Africa when African elites began to emerge. Inspiration for the movement had come originally from Negro intellectuals outside Africa in the British West Indies, the United States, London, and Paris. Their ideas were initially sifted into Africa primarily via West Africans with whom they were able to establish an intellectual rapport. But the West African Pan-Africanists—Nkrumah, Azikiwe, Awolowo, Touré, and Senghor—had no monopoly on the Pan-African concept, which readily found adherents among nationalist leaders from other parts of the continent. Since his days in London when he shared a room with Nkrumah, Kenyatta has espoused the cause. Tom Mboya of Kenya is another leading Pan-Africanist.

In February of this year the PAFMECA powers met at Addis Ababa where they were joined by delegations from Ethiopia, Somalia, Urundi, Nyasaland, Northern Rhodesia, Southern Rhodesia, Mozambique, Republic of South Africa, South West Africa, Basutoland, Bechuanaland, and Swaziland. Although there were no representatives from the Congo (Leopoldville) or Angola, both countries were regarded as within the sphere of conference interest. A major move at the opening of the meeting was the inclusion of South Africa in the official name of the organization, thus changing it from PAFMECA to PAFMECSA.

Further indication of the importance attached to southern Africa was the election of Kenneth Kaunda of Northern Rhodesia as chairman of the organization for 1962. Kaunda was successful in attracting wide support for his country's drive for independence. He made clear that unless Africans won major concessions towards African rule in 1962, his party would forsake its commitment to nonviolence in 1963.

Observers at the Addis Ababa Conference gained the impression that the area stretching from Ethiopia southwards has a better chance of achieving a working unity than any other region in Africa. The political orientation of PAFMECSA covers a wide range from leftist extremism to a neutralism which is not unsympathetic to the West. As of the present, the prevailing attitude appears to be one of determination in opposition to the remnants of colonialism in southern Africa combined with moderation in the general view toward Africa's present day problems.

Economic and Technical Assistance Organizations

A multitude of agencies are engaged in channeling economic and technical assistance to the emerging nations of Africa. Some of these are instruments of European governments established to channel aid to their colonial territories or associated states. Numerous multilateral agencies, such as the International Bank for Reconstruction and Development, are also supporting African development programs.

Because of their exclusively African orientation the following organizations deserve mention in this catalogue: the Economic Commission for Africa (ECA); the Commission for Technical Cooperation in Africa South of the Sahara (CCTA); and the Scientific Council for Africa South of the Sahara (CSA). The latter two groups are frequently referred to jointly as the CCTA/CSA. They share a small permanent secretariat with offices in several European and African capitals. While none of these three organizations is a "bloc" grouping, they are cited herein as mechanisms for promoting cooperation between African states.

The Economic Commission for Africa, a regional economic commission of the United Nations, was set up in 1958 with headquarters in Addis Ababa. It is the counterpart of commissions established earlier in Europe (ECE), Latin America (ECLA), and the Far East (ECAFE). Membership in ECA consists of the independent African states as well as those European nations which still administer colonial territories in Africa. Consultative status at ECA's periodic meetings has been granted to many other UN member

States interested in Africa, including both the United States and the Soviet Union, and to numerous UN specialized agencies as well as private organizations. The Commission's permanent secretariat at Addis Ababa with its large staff of international civil servants provides the only effective mechanism on the continent for viewing Africa's economic problems in their entirety.

The CCTA/CSA was created in 1950 after prolonged discussion among the European colonial powers of the need for coordinating their policies and programs of technical assistance to Africa—CCTA as a device for coordinating the administration of technical assistance and CSA as a scientific council composed of recognized experts competent to advise CCTA on a non-political basis. Both groups originally had representation from four European colonial countries, Great Britain, France, Belgium, and Portugal. African membership was confined to South Africa and the two Rhodesias (after 1953, the Federation), the only sub-Saharan countries considered to be in a position to provide technical and scientific assistance to other African nations. All of the newly-independent African states have now joined the CCTA/CSA, and the founding colonial countries are assuming an associate status. Pressure has been applied by a number of the newer members of the organization to force South Africa to withdraw its membership. The division of functions between ECA and CCTA/CSA is far from precise. In general, ECA tends to be an economic planning and programing organization while CCTA/CSA is chiefly an operational agency actively engaged in technical and scientific projects.

Conclusions

Of the new states of Africa none has sought to play a more aggressive role in international affairs than Ghana. Indeed, Nkrumah's very efforts to seize the leadership of the Pan-African movement have spurred the Brazzaville and Monrovia groupings to counter with a drive toward African unity which, in comparison with Nkrumah's Pan-Africanism, is less political and more functional, less continental and more regional, less precipitate and more gradual.

The outcome of the struggle for power between various blocs and groupings in Africa is anything but clear. Meaningful progress toward sustained unity of any kind will be difficult at best. Even the most extreme nationalist recognizes that Congo-type chaos brings benefit to none except the communists who exploit it to their own ends. But just as many African leaders oppose Nkrumah's flirtations with the Soviets, they will also strongly oppose efforts by the Western nations to interfere in their affairs or to establish areas of special influence.

PARTICIPATION OF AFRICAN GROUPINGS IN MAJOR ORGANIZATIONS AND CONFERENCES

	Ghana-Guinea-Mali Union	Casablanca Group	Conference of Independent African States	All-African Peoples Conference (Cairo)	AATUF (Casablanca) Founders	Belgrade Conference	Conseil d'Entente	Brazzaville Group	Monrovia Group	Lagos Conference	West African Customs Union	Equatorial African Customs Union	CCTA/CSA	Economic Commission for Africa	East African Common Services Organization (4)	PAFMECA
Algeria (FLN)		X		X	X	X								X		
Ghana	X	X	X	X	X	X							(3)	X		
Guinea	X	X	X	X	X	X								X		
Mali	X	X		X	X	X					X			X		
Morocco		X	X	X	X	X								X		
U.A.R.		X	X	X	X									X		
Cameroun			O					X	X	X		X	X	X		
Central African Republic								X	X	X		X	X	X		
Chad								X	X	X		X	X	X		
Congo Republic (Brazzaville)								X	X	X		X	X	X		
Dahomey							X	X	X	X	X		X	X		
Gabon								X	X	X		X	X	X		
Ivory Coast				X			X	X	X	X	X		X	X		
Malagasy								X	X	X			X	X		
Mauritania								X	X	X	X		X	X		
Niger				X			X	X	X	X	X		X	X		
Senegal				X				X	X	X	X		X	X		
Togo									X	X						
Upper Volta	(1)			X			X	X	X	X	X		X	X		
Republic of the Congo									X				X	X		
Ethiopia			X	X		X			X				X	X		
Liberia			X	X					X	X			X	X		
Libya		(2)							X				X	X		
Nigeria			X	X					X	X			X	X		
Sierra Leone			O	X					X	X			X	X		
Somalia			X	X					X	X			X	X		
Republic of South Africa				X									X	X		
Sudan			X	X									X	X		
Tunisia			X	X	X	X			X				X	X		
Angola			O	X												
Kenya			O	X											X	X
Mozambique				X												
Nyasaland			O	X										X		X
Rhodesia, North			O	X										X		O
Rhodesia, South			O	X										X		
Ruanda-Urundi			O	X												
South West Africa			O	X												
Tanganyika			O						X						X	X
Uganda			O												X	X
Zanzibar			O												O	X

Countries are listed on left in four groups as follows: (1) Casablanca powers; (2) Brazzaville (OAMCE) powers plus Togo; (3) other independent African nations; (4) territories or countries which have not yet achieved independence. Spanish territories and most of the Portuguese territories are not listed.

X = indicates membership or official participation.
O = indicates observer or associate status.

References:
(1) Upper Volta has a customs union agreement with Ghana.
(2) Libya attended first Casablanca group meeting.
(3) Ghana joined the CCTA/CSA and withdrew.
(4) East African Common Services Organization—a projected outgrowth of East Africa High Commission.
These listings are based on information of relatively recent date but are subject to revision.

Many Africans outside of the ex-French areas have come to regard the association of these areas with France and the Common Market as an impediment to the cause of broader African unity. As negotiations for British entry into the market have proceeded, it has become increasingly apparent that one of the principal hurdles to be overcome at Brussels is the opposition of African nationalists to the concept of a Eurafrica which implies special, if not imperial, privilege for Europe.

In the months immediately ahead, the Monrovia group and the East African nations will both be seeking to consolidate the progress they have thus far made toward unification. All African groupings will be anxious to demonstrate their commitment to the anticolonial cause by vigorous opposition to any effort on the part of Europeans to block further independence movements in southern Africa. This will be a crucial period in determining whether Africa is to be spared more violence in its progress toward unity.*

---

*John Marcum, "How Wide is the Gap between Casablanca and Monrovia?" *Africa Report,* January 1962; "West Africa: Now Freedom," *The Economist,* January 20, 1962; Frederick H. Gareau, "Bloc Politics in West Africa," *Orbis,* Winter, 1962; and Barbara Jackson, "Free Africa and the Common Market," *Foreign Affairs,* April 1962. The weekly magazine *West Africa* published in London carries numerous articles dealing with this subject.

SELECTED BIBLIOGRAPHY

AFRICA AND INTERNATIONAL ORGANIZATION

CAROL A. JOHNSON

SARA S. RUSSELL

I. AFRICA AND THE UNITED NATIONS

"Africa at the U.N.—Thoughts on Emergent Continent." *Africa Today,* October 1960.

"Africa's Role in United Nations." *Africa World,* April 1960, p. 4.

"Africans at the UN." *West Africa,* October 1, 1960 (No. 2261), p. 1125.

"Afro-Asia Asserts Itself." *West Africa,* September 24, 1960 (No. 2260), p. 1075.

"Agenda for Africa." *West Africa,* August 15, 1959 (No. 2202), p. 593.

Arden-Clarke, Charles. "South West Africa, the Union, and the United Nations." *African Affairs,* January 1960 (Vol. 59, No. 234), p. 26–35.

Beer, Max. "Die Vereinigten Nationen und Africa." *Schweizer Monatschafte,* July 1961 (41st Year, No. 4), p. 370–379.

Chidzero, B. T. G. *Tanganyika and International Trusteeship.* New York, Oxford University Press, 1961. 286 p.

Cohen, Sir Andrew. "The New Africa and the United Nations," in Legum, Colin, *Africa: A Handbook to the Continent.* London, Anthony Blond, Ltd., 1961; New York, Frederick A. Praeger, 1962; p. 491–499.

Cottrell, W. F. "The U.N. and Africa." *Annals of the American Academy of Political and Social Sciences,* July 1956 (Vol. 306), p. 55–61.

Gillespie, Joan. "Africa's Voice at the United Nations." *Africa Special Report,* June 1959 (Vol. 4, No. 6), p. 13–14.

Houser, George M. "U.S. at U.N.—Cause for Concern." *Africa Today,* January 1961 (Vol. 8, No. 1), p. 5–6, 10–11.

Irvine, Keith. "African Nationalism and the U.N." *Current History,* June 1960 (Vol. 38, No. 226).

Jack, Homer A. "The 'African Assembly.'" *Africa Today,* November 1960 (Vol. 7, No. 7), p. 9–11, 14.

Landis, Elisabeth S. "1960 Agenda, Africa—UN Report." *Africa Today,* October 1960 (Vol. 7, No. 6), p. 11–12.

————. "UN Vote on African Issues at 15th General Assembly." *Africa Today,* January 1961 (Vol. 8, No. 1), p. 7–9.

"L'évolution de la crise congolaise de septembre 1960 à avril 1961." *Chronique de Politique Etrangère,* September–November 1961 (Vol. 14, Nos. 5–6), p. 565–1154.

Marlow, Will. "Afro-Asian Bloc in the United Nations." *Middle Eastern Affairs,* November 1957 (Vol. 8, No. 11), p. 372–377.

Quaison-Sackey, Alex. "Progress Toward Charter Aims in the World's Dependent Territories." *United Nations Review,* May 1960 (Vol. 6, No. 11), p. 8–12.

Rivkin, Arnold. "The U.N. in Africa." *West Africa,* Part 1, March 26, 1960 (No. 2234), p. 353; Part 2, April 2, 1960 (No. 2235), p. 376; Part 3, April 9, 1960 (No. 2236), p. 405.

Sears, Mason. "The Congo, Africa, and the U.N." *Africa Today,* September 1960 (Vol. 7, No. 5), p. 14–15.

"The U.N. in Africa." *West Africa,* March 26, 1960 (No. 2234), p. 337.

Touré, Sékou. "Call for Real Application of Right to Self-Determination in Africa." *United Nations Review,* December 1959 (Vol. 6, No. 6), p. 20–21.

"U.N. Concentrates on Africa." *West Africa*, December 10, 1960 (No. 2271), p. 1409.

Watt, David. "The UN and the Small Nations." *New Leader*, March 6, 1961 (Vol. 44, No. 10), p. 6–7.

"West Africans Support U.N." *West Africa*, August 27, 1960 (No. 2256), p. 975.

Wilcox, F. O. "New Africa and the U.N." Department of State *Bulletin*, April 18, 1960 (Vol. 42, No. 1086), p. 589.

II. AFRICAN POLITICAL AND REGIONAL GROUPINGS

GENERAL

"Africa from Accra." *West Africa*, August 20, 1960 (No. 2255), p. 925.

"Africa from Lagos." *West Africa*, August 27, 1960 (No. 2256), p. 956.

"Africa's Hour." *The Economist*, September 10, 1960 (Vol. 196, No. 6107), p. 701–702.

"Africa's Year of Revolution." *West Africa*, December 31, 1960 (No. 2274), p. 1469–1470.

"As M. Sékou Touré Sees It." *The Economist*, July 23, 1960 (Vol. 196, No. 6100), p. 377–378.

"Balkan Africa." *The Economist*, August 13, 1960 (Vol. 196, No. 6103), p. 618–619.

Bourguiba, Habib. "The Outlook for Africa." *International Affairs*, October 1961 (Vol. 37, No. 4), p. 425–431.

Coleman, James S. "The Politics of Sub-Sahara Africa," in Almond, Gabriel A. and James S. Coleman, eds., *The Politics of the Developing Areas*. Princeton, Princeton University Press, 1960, p. 247–368.

"Confederate States of Africa?" *The Economist*, January 16, 1960 (Vol. 194, No. 6073), p. 192.

"Dangerous Divisions in Africa." *West Africa*, November 12, 1960 (No. 2267), p. 1269.

Dia, Mamadou, *The African Nations and World Solidarity*. New York, Praeger, 1961. 145 p.

Elias, T. O. *Government and Politics in Africa*. London, Asia Publishing House, 1961. xv + 228 p.

Francolini, Bruno. "Il problema politico dell'Africa nera." *Studi Politici*, January–March 1961 (8th Year, No. 1), p. 27–46.

Gareau, Frederick H. "Bloc Politics in West Africa." *Orbis*, Winter 1962 (Vol. 5, No. 4), p. 470–488.

Hamon, Leo. "Formes et perspectives de la democratie en Afrique." *Civilisations*, 1961 (Vol. 11, No. 3), p. 245–264.

Houser, George M. "The Changing Face of African Nationalism." *Africa Today*, April 1960 (Vol. 7, No. 2), p. 9–10.

"Houphouet-Boigny and the Two Africas." *West Africa*, November 18, 1961 (No. 2320), p. 1265–1266.

Houphouet-Boigny, Félix. "Les chances de l'Afrique." *Revue Politique et Parlémentaire*, July 1961 (63d Year, No. 714), p. 3–11.

"Independent Africa and the Congo." *West Africa*, July 16, 1960 (No. 2250), p. 785.

"Is Africa Divided?" *West Africa*, February 10, 1962 (No. 2332), p. 141.

Kloman, Erasmus H., Jr. "An African Program for the Africans." *New Leader*, March 13, 1961 (Vol. 44, No. 11), p. 14–17.

Lewis, Arthur W. "Sources of Tension in West Africa." *Africa Special Report*, September 1960 (Vol. 5, No. 9), p. 5–6.

"Many Africas: A Continent in Turmoil." *Journal of International Affairs*, 1961 (Vol. 15, No. 1), p. 5–76.

Mars, Louis. "L'Organisation des Nations Africaines." *Communauté France-Eurafrique*, September 1961 (13th Year, No. 124), p. 2–4.

"Nigeria, 'No Surrender of Sovereignty.' " *Africa Digest*, February 1960 (Vol. 7, No. 4), p. 135.

"Nkrumah on 'Union of Africa States.' " *Africa Digest*, February 1960 (Vol. 7, No. 4), p. 132–133.

"No Black Pawns." *The Economist*, June 3, 1961 (Vol. 199, No. 6145), p. 975–976.

Perin, François. "La crise congolaise et les institutions Africaines." *Civilisations*, 1961 (Vol. 11, No. 3), p. 281–295.

"Prospects for African Unity." *West Africa*, December 30, 1961 (No. 2326), p. 1433–1434.

Rivkin, Arnold. "Independent Africa and Congo." *West Africa*, Part 1, November 26, 1960 (No. 2269), p. 1341; Part 2, December 3, 1960 (No. 2270), p. 1368.

Rothchild, Donald S. *Toward Unity in Africa: A Study of Federalism in British Africa.* Washington, D.C., Public Affairs Press, 1960. vii + 224 p.

Segal, Ronald and others. *Political Africa.* New York, Praeger, 1961. 475 p.

"Solid Black." *The Economist*, August 19, 1961 (Vol. 200, No. 6156), p. 699.

"The Two Accra Conferences." *The World Today*, April 1959 (Vol. 15, No. 4), p. 147–156.

"United States Diplomat Discusses: 'The Challenge of the Hour.'" (Condensed text of an address by Joseph C. Satterthwaite.) *Africa Special Report*, March 1959 (Vol. 4, No. 3), p. 9–12.

Wallerstein, Immanuel. *Africa, the Politics of Independence.* New York, Vintage Books, 1961. 167 p. + appendix + bibliographical note.

"West Africa: Now Freedom." *The Economist*, January 20, 1962 (Vol. 202, No. 6178), p. 203–206.

Yacé, Philippe. "Les chances de l'Eurafrique." *Communauté France-Eurafrique*, July–August 1961 (13th Year, No. 123), p. 5–8.

PAN-AFRICANISM

Azikiwe, Nnamdi. *The Future of Pan-Africanism.* (An address given by the Governor-General of the Federation of Nigeria in London, August 1961.) Published by the Nigeria High Commission, London.

Decraene, Philippe. "West African Unity." *Africa South*, January–March 1960 (Vol. 4, No. 2), p. 92–99.

"Dr. Azikiwe on Pan-Africa." *West Africa*, August 19, 1961 (No. 2307), p. 925.

Hambly, Wilfred D. "A United Africa? Racial and Economic Obstacles to Political Unity." *African World*, November 1960, p. 7–9.

Hempstone, Smith. *Africa—Angry Young Giant.* New York, Praeger, 1961. 664 p.

"Katanga and Pan-Africa." *West Africa*, July 23, 1960 (No. 2251), p. 813–814.

Legum, Colin. *Pan-Africanism: A Short Political Guide.* New York, Praeger, 1961. 288 p.

——. "The Roots of Pan-Africanism," in Legum, Colin, *Africa: A Handbook to the Continent.* London, Anthony Blond, Ltd., 1961; New York, Frederick A. Praeger, 1962; p. 452–462.

Padmore, George. *Pan-Africanism or Communism?* New York, Roy Publishers, 1956. 463 p.

"Prospects for Pan-Africa." *West Africa*, December 6, 1958 (No. 2173), p. 1153–1154.

"Rise of the Pan-African Movement." *Africa Special Report*, April 1958 (Vol. 3, No. 4), p. 5–9.

ALL-AFRICAN PEOPLE'S CONFERENCES

GENERAL

Cone, L. Winston. "Ghana's African and World Relations." *India Quarterly*, July–September 1961 (Vol. 17, No. 3), p. 258–276.

Wheeler, Elizabeth H. "Guideposts to African Aspirations." *Free World Forum*, Spring 1961 (Vol. 11, No. 1), p. 35–39.

FIRST ALL-AFRICAN PEOPLE'S CONFERENCE (ACCRA)

"Accra People's Conference Opens." *West Africa*, December 6, 1958 (No. 2173), p. 1167.

"Africa Lifts Its Voice." *Political Affairs*, February 1959 (Vol. 39, No. 2), p. 1–8.

"African People at Accra." *West Africa*, December 13, 1958 (No. 2174), p. 1191.

"Annual All-African People's Conferences." *West Africa*, December 20, 1958 (No. 2175), p. 1215.

Duncan, Pat. "Violence or Non-Violence. Division Between East and West?" *Africa Special Report*, February 1959 (Vol. 4, No. 2), p. 7–8.

"Ghana's All-Africa Conference in December." *West Africa*, September 20, 1958 (No. 2162), p. 903.

Hughes, John. "The Accra Meeting." *New Leader*, January 12, 1959 (Vol. 42, No. 2), p. 6–7.

Jack, Homer A. "Russian Scholars Lead Seven-Man Observer Team." *Africa Special Report*, February 1959 (Vol. 4, No. 2), p. 8.

Marcum, John. "French-Speaking Africa at Accra." *Africa Special Report*, February 1959 (Vol. 4, No. 2), p. 9–10.

———. "The Spirit of Accra." *New Leader*, March 2, 1959 (Vol. 42, No. 9), p. 11–12.

"People's Conference Plans Permanent Body." *Africa Special Report*, February 1959 (Vol. 4, No. 2), p. 3–7.

"Text of Resolutions of First All-African People's Conference." Reproduced in *Current History*, July 1959 (Vol. 37, No. 215), p. 41–46.

"The All-African People's Conference." *Africa Today*, December 1959 (Vol. 6, No. 6), p. 3, 21.

SECOND ALL-AFRICAN PEOPLE'S CONFERENCE (TUNIS)

"African Voices in Tunis." *West Africa*, February 13, 1960 (No. 2228), p. 117.

"Africans in Congress." *The Economist*, Part I, February 6, 1960 (Vol. 194, No. 6076), p. 534; Part II, February 20, 1960 (Vol. 194, No. 6078), p. 728–730.

"All-Africa at Tunis." *West Africa*, February 6, 1960 (No. 2227), p. 141–142.

"All Africa People's Conference at Tunis." *West Africa*, February 6, 1960 (No. 2227), p. 143.

"All-African Peoples at Tunis." *West Africa*, January 30, 1960 (No. 2226), p. 130.

"All-African People's Conference Convenes in Tunis." *Africa Report*, January 1960 (Vol. 5, No. 1), p. 6.

Hahn, Lorna. "Africans Meet in Tunis." *New Leader*, February 8, 1960 (Vol. 43, No. 6), p. 8.

Hoskyns, Catherine. "Tunis Diary: An Impression of the Second All-African People's Conference." *Africa South*, July–September 1960 (Vol. 4, No. 4), p. 104–111.

Houser, George M. "The Changing Face of African Nationalism." *Africa Today*, April 1960 (Vol. 7, No. 2), p. 9–10.

"Tunis Conference." *Africa Digest*, February 1960 (Vol. 7, No. 4), p. 137.

"Tunis Conference Ends on Militant Note." *Africa Report*, February 1960 (Vol. 5, No. 2), p. 13.

THIRD ALL-AFRICAN PEOPLE'S CONFERENCE (CAIRO)

"All Africa People's Condemn Neo-Colonialism." *West Africa*, April 8, 1961 (No. 2288), p. 389.

Houser, George M. "At Cairo—The Third All-African People's Conference." *Africa Today*, April 1961 (Vol. 8, No. 4), p. 11–13.

BRAZZAVILLE POWERS

"African Eleven." *The Economist*, December 1960 (Vol. 197, No. 6123), p. 1388, 1390.

"African Leaders Convene at Rival 'Summits.'" *Africa Report*, January 1961 (Vol. 6, No. 1), p. 11.

"An Algerian Summit." *The Economist*, October 29, 1960 (Vol. 197, No. 6114), p. 435.

"Brazzaville Decisions." *West Africa*, December 24, 1960 (No. 2273), p. 1451.

d'Arboussier, Gabriel. "Youandé: douze peuples unis pour le meilleur et pour le pire." *Communauté France-Eurafrique*, April 1961 (13th Year, No. 120), p. 4–5.

Deljean, Thomas. "Tananarine: Les Douze recherchent cohésion et efficacité." *Communauté France-Eurafrique*, September 1961 (13th Year, No. 124), p. 27–28.

"French Africans at Brazzaville." *West Africa*, December 17, 1960 (No. 2272), p. 1423.

"French Soldiers and Africa." *West Africa*, April 8, 1961 (No. 2288), p. 367.

"French-Speaking States Seek Common Policies." *Africa Digest*, December 1960 (Vol. 5, No. 12), p. 12.

"Le Vent de Changement." *West Africa*, December 31, 1960 (No. 2274), p. 1471.

Lętocha, Tadeusz. "Panstwa Brazzaville." *Sprawy Międznynarodowe*, November 1961 (Vol. 14, No. 11), p. 52–68.

Pick, Hella. "The Brazzaville Twelve." *Africa South*, April–June 1961 (Vol. 5, No. 3), p. 76–84.

——. "The Brazzaville Twelve and How They Came to Be." *Africa Report*, May 1961 (Vol. 6, No. 5), p. 2, 8, 12, 15.

"Strictly Business at Yaondé." *West Africa*, April 8, 1961 (No. 2288), p. 366.

"The Two Congos in Brazzaville." *West Africa*, December 24, 1960 (No. 2273), p. 1442.

Willane, Omar. "L'Organisation Africaine et Malgache de Coopération Economique et son incidence sur le problème des échanges." *Communauté France-Eurafrique*, July–August 1961 (13th Year, No. 123), p. 22–24.

CASABLANCA POWERS

"African Leaders Convene at Rival 'Summits!'" *Africa Report*, January 1961 (Vol. 6, No. 1), p. 11.

"African Summit Meeting." *West Africa*, January 7, 1961 (No. 2275), p. 11.

"Casablanca and Monrovia." *West Africa*, July 29, 1961 (No. 2304), p. 817.

"Casablanca States Reject Lagos Invitations." *West Africa*, January 27, 1962 (No. 2330), p. 102.

Ellis, Harry B. "Failure at Casablanca." *New Leader*, February 20, 1961 (Vol. 44, No. 8), p. 14–15.

"Is Africa Divided?" *West Africa*, February 10, 1962 (No. 2332), p. 141.

"No Surprises at Casablanca Decision." *West Africa*, January 27, 1962 (No. 2330), p. 95.

"Plan for Pan-African Airways." *West Africa*, November 4, 1961 (No. 2318), p. 1233.

"Road from Casablanca." *The Economist*, January 14, 1961 (Vol. 198, No. 6125), p. 121–122.

Roberts, Margaret. "Casablanca 'Summit.'" *Venture*, February 1961 (Vol. 13, No. 2), p. 1–2.

——. "Pan-Africa and the Congo." *West Africa*, January 14, 1961 (No. 2276), p. 31.

——. "Summitry at Casablanca." *Africa South*, April–June 1961 (Vol. 3, No. 3), p. 60–71.

"Transcending Differences." *Africa Today*, February 1961 (Vol. 8, No. 2), p. 8–9.

AFRICAN ECONOMIC COMMITTEE

"Casablanca and Monrovia." *West Africa*, July 29, 1961 (No. 2304), p. 830.

"Casablanca Economists Discuss Customs Union." *Africa Report*, August 1961 (Vol. 6, No. 8), p. 11–12.

"Conakry." *West Africa*, July 22, 1961 (No. 2303), p. 799.

CONFERENCES OF INDEPENDENT STATES

FIRST CONFERENCE OF INDEPENDENT STATES (ACCRA)

"Accra Parley Demands End to Racialism, Foreign Rule in Africa." *Africa Special Report*, April 1958 (Vol. 3, No. 4), p. 1, 3–4, 10–11.

"Accra's Economic Resolution." *West Africa*, May 10, 1958 (No. 2143), p. 441.

"Accra's International Conference." *West Africa*, March 29, 1958 (No. 2137), p. 290.

"African Explorers in Accra." *West Africa*, April 26, 1958 (No. 2141), p. 385.

"African States Associated." *West Africa*, April 3, 1958 (No. 2138), p. 327.

"Conference of Independent African States, Accra, 15th–22d April, 1958." *New Ghana*, souvenir edition, April 30, 1958 (Vol. 11, No. 9).

"Conference of Independent African States—Declaration." *West Africa*, May 10, 1958 (No. 2143), p. 449.

Conference of Independent African States: Declaration and Resolutions, 22nd April, 1958. Accra, Ghana, Government Printer, 1958.

Conference of Independent African States: Speeches Delivered at the Inaugural Session, 15th April, 1958. Accra, Ghana, Government Printer, 1958.

"Eight States in Accra." *West Africa*, April 12, 1958 (No. 2139), p. 337.

"Implementing Accra Resolutions." *West Africa*, September 6, 1958 (No. 2160), p. 861.

"Independent Africa at Accra." *West Africa*, April 19, 1958 (No. 2140), p. 375.

"Independent Africa in Accra." *West Africa*, April 26, 1958 (No. 2141), p. 387.

Legum, Colin. "Ghana: The Morning After the Accra Conference." *Africa South*, July–September 1958 (Vol. 2, No. 4), p. 82–93.

Official Handbook. Conference of Independent States—April 1958. Accra, Ghana, Government Printer, 1958.

"The Accra Conference." *Africa Today*, May–June 1958 (Vol. 5, No. 3), p. 6–12.

SECOND CONFERENCE OF INDEPENDENT STATES (ADDIS ABABA)

"Addis Ababa Conference." *West Africa*, June 25, 1960 (No. 2247), p. 725.

"African Political Leaders Confer in Addis Ababa." *Africa Report*, July 1960 (Vol. 5, No. 7), p. 5.

"From Accra to Addis." *West Africa*, July 2, 1960 (No. 2248), p. 729.

"Independent African States at Addis Ababa." *West Africa*, June 18, 1960 (No. 2246), p. 697.

Pankhurst, Richard. "Independent African States at Addis Ababa." *West Africa*, Part 1, July 2, 1960 (No. 2248), p. 731; Part 2, July 9, 1960 (No. 2249), p. 769.

CONSEIL DE L'ENTENTE

"Abidjan." *West Africa*, August 20, 1960 (No. 2255), p. 931.

"Abidjan Round-Table." *West Africa*, October 22, 1960 (No. 2263), p. 1195.

Berg, Elliot J. "Economics of Independence." *West Africa*, March 17, 1962 (No. 2337), p. 293.

"Entente States Seek Independence in August." *Africa Special Report*, August 1960 (Vol. 5, No. 8), p. 8–9.

"Entente's Enfant Terrible." *West Africa*, August 26, 1961 (No. 2308), p. 935.

"France to Continue Aid to Four Entente States." *Africa Report*, April 1961 (Vol. 6, No. 4), p. 11.

"Free Trade and Solidarity." *West Africa*, June 6, 1959 (No. 2199), p. 539.

"French-Speaking Tropical Africa Revises Its Political Institutions." *Africa Report*, February 1961 (Vol. 6, No. 2), p. 2, 8.

"Harmony in A.O.F." *West Africa*, June 13, 1959 (No. 2200), p. 559.

"Ouagadougou." *West Africa*, January 14, 1961 (No. 2276), p. 39.

"Progress at Niamey." *West Africa*, April 1, 1961 (No. 2287), p. 347.

"Symbol of the Moderates in Ex-French Africa." *West Africa*, February 4, 1961 (No. 2279), p. 117.

"Vent de Changement." *The Economist*, March 18, 1961 (Vol. 198, No. 6134), p. 1073–1074.

"West African Manoeuvres." *The Economist*, June 25, 1960 (Vol. 195, No. 6096), p. 1345–1346.

EAST AFRICAN COMMON SERVICES ORGANIZATION (FORMERLY EAST AFRICA HIGH COMMISSION)

The Future of East African High Commission Services: Report of the London Discussion, June 1961. London, H.M.S.O., Cmnd. 1433.

GHANA-GUINEA-MALI UNION

"Accra Communiqué Causes Dismay." *West Africa*, May 6, 1961 (No. 2292), p. 495.

Charter for the Union of African States and a Joint Communiqué Issued Later after a Summit Conference between the Leaders of the Union. Accra, Ghana, Government Printing Department, 1961.

"End of an African Frontier." *West Africa*, July 8, 1961 (No. 2301), p. 751.

"Ghana, Guinea and Mali Unite." *West Africa*, December 31, 1960 (No. 2274), p. 1486.

"Ghana-Guinea and the World." *West Africa*, December 6, 1958 (No. 2173), p. 1173.

"Ghana, Guinea, Mali Confer on Union." *Africa Report*, February 1961 (Vol. 6, No. 2), p. 10.

"Ghana, Guinea, Mali Formalize Their Union." *Africa Report*, August 1961 (Vol. 6, No. 8), p. 11.

"Ghana-Guinea Union Proposed." *West Africa*, November 29, 1958 (No. 2172), p. 1143.

"Joint Ghana-Mali Parliament." *West Africa*, December 3, 1960 (No. 2270), p. 1378.

"Mali and Guinea." *West Africa*, May 30, 1959 (No. 2198), p. 515.

"Mali, Ghana, Guinea Sign Union Charter." *Africa Report*, May 1961 (Vol. 6, No. 5), p. 11.

"Nkrumah, Touré, Propose Wider Union." *Africa Special Report*, May 1959 (Vol. 4, No. 5), p. 3–4.

"The Osagyefo and Others." *The Economist*, December 31, 1960 (Vol. 197, No. 6123), p. 1366–1367.

MONROVIA POWERS

MONROVIA CONFERENCE

"African States at Monrovia." *West Africa*, May 13, 1961 (No. 2293), p. 521.

Howe, Russell. "The Monrovia Conference." *Africa Today*, May 1961 (Vol. 8, No. 5), p. 4.

"Independent Africa in Monrovia." *West Africa*, May 20, 1961 (No. 2294), p. 539.

Maffert, Serge. "De Yaoundé à Monrovia à la poursuite de l'unité africaine." *Communauté France-Eurafrique*, April 1961 (13th Year, No. 120), p. 5–7.

————. "Les Résolutions de Monrovia et la Charte de Casablanca." *Communauté France-Eurafrique*, May 1961 (13th Year, No. 121), p. 2–3.

"Monrovia's Full Resolutions." *West Africa*, June 3, 1961 (No. 2296), p. 608.

Opening Speeches, Conference of Heads of African and Malagasy States, Held at the Centennial Pavilion, 8th–12th May 1961. Monrovia, Liberian Information Service, 1961.

"Pan-African Affairs." *Africa Digest*, August 1961 (Vol. 9, No. 1), p. 37.

"Pan-African First Steps." *The Economist*, April 29, 1961 (Vol. 199, No. 6140), p. 454–456.

Resolutions of the Plenary Sessions, Conference of Heads of African and Malagasy States, Held at Monrovia City Hall, 8th–12th May 1961. Monrovia, Liberian Information Service, 1961.

Sale, J. Kirk. "Power Struggle in Africa." *New Leader*, June 19, 1961 (Vol. 44, No. 25), p. 12–13.

"The Co-operators." *The Economist*, May 20, 1961 (Vol. 199, No. 6143), p. 766.

"The Monrovia Conference." *Africa Report*, June 1961 (Vol. 6, No. 6), p. 5.

"The Monrovia Conference." *Présence Africaine*, 1961 (Vol. 9, No. 37), p. 193–199.

LAGOS CONFERENCE

"African Unity Now." *West Africa*, January 20, 1962 (No. 2329), p. 57–58.

"La Conférence de Lagos . . . " *Etudes Congolais*, 1962 (No. 3), p. 20–23.

"Lagos and Addis Ababa Conferences." *Asia & Africa Review*, March 1962 (Vol. 2, No. 3), p. 6.

"Lagos Battle Lost?" *West Africa*, January 27, 1962 (No. 2330), p. 87.

"Lagos Summit on January 25." *West Africa*, December 16, 1961 (No. 2324), p. 1394.

"Monrovians Muddle Through." *The Economist*, February 3, 1962 (Vol. 202, No. 6180), p. 431–432.

"Now, Freedom." *The Economist*, January 20, 1962 (Vol. 202, No. 6178), p. 203–206.

Roberts, Margaret. "What Price for African Unity?" *African Trade and Development*, March 1962 (Vol. 4, No. 3), p. 9, 16.

Sterne, Joseph R. L. "The Lagos Conference." *Africa Report*, February 1962 (Vol. 7, No. 2), p. 3–6, 23.

"Success and Failure at Lagos." *West Africa*, February 3, 1962 (No. 2331), p. 113–114.

"The Lagos Decisions." *West Africa*, February 10, 1962 (No. 2332), p. 149.

"What Happened at Lagos?" *West Africa*, February 3, 1962 (No. 2331), p. 113.

PAN-AFRICAN FREEDOM MOVEMENT IN EAST, CENTRAL, AND SOUTH AFRICA (PAFMECSA, FORMERLY PAFMECA)

"A New Nigeria?" *The Economist*, October 29, 1960 (Vol. 197, No. 6114), p. 432, 435.

"Africa: Southward March." *The Economist*, February 10, 1962 (Vol. 202, No. 6181), p. 537–538.

"East Africans Call for Self-Government." *Africa Special Report,* September 1959 (Vol. 4, No. 9), p. 2.

"Embryonic Alliance Emerges at PAFMECSA Conference." *Africa Report,* March 1962 (Vol. 7, No. 3), p. 14.

Kiano, Gikonyo. "The Pan-African Freedom Movement of East and Central Africa." *Africa Today,* September 1959 (Vol. 6, No. 4), p. 11–14.

"Lagos and Addis Ababa Conferences." *Asia & Africa Review,* March 1962 (Vol. 2, No. 3), p. 6–7.

"Mr. Kaunda Heads Pan-Africa Group." *East Africa and Rhodesia,* February 15, 1962 (Vol. 39, No. 1949), p. 598.

"Out of Step." *The Economist,* September 3, 1960 (Vol. 196, No. 6106), p. 979–980.

"Pan-African Conference." *Africa Digest,* November–December 1958 (Vol. 6, No. 3), p. 90–91.

"Pan-African Freedom Movement." *East Africa and Rhodesia,* September 17, 1959 (Vol. 36, No. 1823), p. 58.

"Summer Saneness." *The Economist,* July 8, 1961 (Vol. 200, No. 6150), p. 124.

SPECIAL CONFERENCES

MONROVIA CONFERENCE ON ALGERIA

Africa Digest, September 1959 (Vol. 7, No. 1), p. 38, and November 1959 (Vol. 7, No. 2), p. 68.

"African States United on Algeria." *Africa Special Report,* August 1959 (Vol. 4, No. 7), p. 2–4.

Gillespie, Joan. "Africa Conclave." *New Leader,* September 7, 1959 (Vol. 42, No. 32), p. 10–12.

SANNIQUELLIE CONFERENCE

Africa Digest, November 1959 (Vol. 7, No. 2), p. 68.

Africa Special Report, August 1958 (Vol. 4, No. 7), p. 3–4.

First West African Summit Conference, Held at Sanniquellie, Central Province, Liberian Hinterland, July 15–19, 1959. Monrovia, Liberian Information Service. 32 p.

"West African 'Summit.' " *West Africa,* August 15, 1959 (No. 2202), p. 600.

III. AFRICA AND EUROPE

BRITISH COMMONWEALTH

"A Bunch of Keys." *The Economist,* March 4, 1961 (Vol. 198, No. 6132), p. 825–826.

Assistance from the United Kingdom for Overseas Development. HM Treasury, Cmnd. 974, March 1960.

Austin, Dennis. *West Africa and the Commonwealth.* London, Penguin Books, 1957, 124 p.

"Britain, Africa and Europe." *West Africa,* June 24, 1961 (No. 2299), p. 677–678.

"Britain's New Frontier." *The Economist,* July 22, 1961 (Vol. 200, No. 6152), p. 317–318.

"Commonwealth and EEC." *West Africa,* November 4, 1961 (No. 2318), p. 1217.

"Commonwealth Approaches." *The Economist,* December 1961 (Vol. 200, No. 6173), p. 1129.

"Commonwealth Relations." *West Africa,* June 10, 1961 (No. 2297), p. 629.

"Consulting Room." *The Economist,* December 2, 1961 (Vol. 201, No. 6171), p. 878–879.

Crabbé, Raoul. "La Grande Bretagne et le Commonwealth." *Eurafrica,* June 1961 (5th Year, No. 5), p. 22–23.

"Ghana and the Commonwealth." *West Africa,* November 18, 1961 (No. 2320), p. 1265.

"Redrawing the Commonwealth." *West Africa,* May 21, 1960 (No. 2242), p. 561–562.

"Roads to Rome." *The Economist,* June 17, 1961 (Vol. 199, No. 6147), p. 1203–1204.

"Think Again." *The Economist,* October 7, 1961 (Vol. 201, No. 6163), p. 22.

"U.K. Commonwealth Investment." *West Africa,* November 7, 1959 (No. 2214), p. 950.

Younger, Kenneth. "Reflections on Africa and the Commonwealth." *The World Today*, March 1962 (Vol. 18, No. 3), p. 121–129.

EUROPEAN ECONOMIC COMMUNITY

"A Colloquium at Bari." *West Africa*, July 8, 1961 (No. 2301), p. 739.

"Africa and the European Common Market." *West Africa*, January 10, 1959 (No. 2178), p. 41.

"Africa and the EEC: Prospects for 1962." *Africa Report* (Vol. 6, No. 8), p. 7.

"African Advantages for 'The Six' over 'The Seven.'" *West Africa*, April 2, 1960 (No. 2235), p. 381; and April 9, 1960 (No. 2236), p. 403.

"Africans and the Common Market." *West Africa*, June 24, 1961 (No. 2299), p. 683.

"Another Common Market Question." *West Africa*, June 25, 1960 (No. 2247), p. 702.

Bielfeldt, Hans. "Aspekte der wirtschaftlichen Entwicklung in Africa." *Schweizer Monatschefte* (41st Year, No. 4), July 1961, p. 417–425.

Bots, Maurice. "L'Association des Pays Africains au Marché Commun." *Eurafrica*, January 1962 (6th Year, No. 1), p. 40–41.

————. "L'Europe des Six offre sa collaboration à l'Afrique des Seize." *Eurafrica*, August 1961 (5th Year, No. 7), p. 21–22.

"Common Market Association Prolonged?" *West Africa*, March 3, 1962 (No. 2335), p. 235.

"Common Market Consolidates African Ties." *West Africa*, February 4, 1961 (No. 2279), p. 133.

"Common Market Dilemmas." *West Africa*, March 17, 1962 (No. 2337), p. 282.

Cousté, Pierre Bernard. *L'Association des Pays d'Outre-Mer à la Communauté Économique Européenne.* Paris, Libraires Techniques, 1959. 286 p.

Decreane, Philippe. "Les Etats Africaines veulent maintenir et renforcer l'Association avec l'Europe des Six." *Communauté France-Eurafrique*, June 1961 (13th Year, No. 1220), p. 11–12.

Delagneau, Bernard. *L'Association des Pays d'Outre-Mer à la Communauté Économique Européenne, son Incidence sur les exportations des Pays d'Outre Mer.* Louvain, Dewailer, 1961. 500 p.

Dumon, Frédéric. *La Communauté Franco-Afro-Malgache.* Brussels, Université Libre de Bruxelles, Institut de Socologie Solvay, 1960. 294 p.

Dupeyron, Jean-François. "Encore de serieuses difficultés à résoudre pour associer les Pays d'Outre-Mer au Marché Commun." *Communauté France-Eurafrique*, October 1961 (13th Year, No. 125), p. 14–15.

————. "L'Association des pays d'Outre-Mer au Marché Commun est un acte politique." *Communauté France-Eurafrique*, December 1961—January 1962 (13th Year, No. 127), p. 4–5.

————. "Quand 142 Parlementaires Européens et 103 Parlementaires Africains tournent ensemble la page de colonialisme." *Communauté France-Eurafrique*, June 1961 (13th Year, No. 122), p. 13–14.

"Eurafrica." *West Africa*, May 2, 1959 (No. 2194), p. 411.

"Eurafrica and Their Africa." *The Economist*, November 25, 1961 (Vol. 201, No. 6170), p. 734–735.

"European Market Menace?" *West Africa*, August 12, 1961 (No. 2306), p. 873–874.

Ibouanga, Isaac. "Face à la Communauté Economique Européenne." *Communauté France-Eurafrique*, June 1961 (13th Year, No. 122), p. 14–15.

"Is the Common Market Dangerous?" *West Africa*, June 11, 1960 (No. 2245), p. 645.

Jackson, Barbara Ward. "Free Africa and the Common Market." *Foreign Affairs*, April 1962 (Vol. 40, No. 3), p.419–430.

"Le Marché Commun et l'Afrique." *Eurafrica*, June 1961 (5th Year, No. 5), p. 12–17.

Lemaignen, L. "Le 'New Look' du Marché Commun à l'égard de l'Afrique." *Eurafrica*, June 1961 (5th Year, No. 5), p. 41.

"Les investissements dans les Pays d'Outre-Mer associés à la Communauté Européenne." Brussels, European Economic Community, July 22, 1959.

"New Partnership with African Countries." *Bulletin from the European Community*, July 1961 (No. 48), p. 4–5.

Nkrumah, Kwame. "What's Wrong with the Common Market?" *West Africa*, July 15, 1961 (No. 2302), p. 763.

"Outer Seven v. Inner Six." *West Africa,* November 21, 1959 (No. 2216), p. 1007.

Pillay, V. "The European Economic Community and Africa." *Africa South,* July–September 1958 (Vol. 2, No. 4), p. 76–81.

Rabemananjara, Jacques. "Un moteur particulièrement efficace: L'Association des Etats d'Afrique et d'Europe." *Communauté France-Eurafrique,* December 1961—January 1962 (13th Year, No. 127), p. 2–3.

Rawlings, E. H. "Africa and the Common Market." *African World,* November 1960, p. 10.

Razafimbahiny, J. "Jouer le jeu, oui, mais tous ensemble." *Communauté France-Eurafrique,* June 1961 (13th Year, No. 122), p. 16–17.

Rivkin, Arnold. "EEC and Africa." *West Africa,* Part 1, February 25, 1961 (No. 2282), p. 203; Part 2, March 4, 1961 (No. 2283), p. 241; Part 3, March 11, 1961 (No. 2284), p. 269.

Rossi, André. "Le Marché Commun et l'Association des Pays et Territoires d'Outre-Mer." *Communauté France-Eurafrique,* September 1959 (11th Year, No. 104), p. 16–17.

"Should African Exports be Protected?" *West Africa,* December 16, 1961 (No. 2324), p. 1379.

"Six and Sixteen." *The Economist,* July 1, 1961 (Vol. 200, No. 6149), p. 47–48.

The Impact of the European Economic Community on African Trade. UN Document E/CN.14/29 and Add.1, November 20, 1959. 25 p. + appendix.

"The 6 and the 16." *West Africa,* July 8, 1961 (No. 2301), p. 749.

"The Six, the Seven and Africa." *West Africa,* May 27, 1961 (No. 2295), p. 571.

Vistosi, Gianfranco. "La Cee e i territori d'oltremare." *Civitas,* August–September 1961 (12th Year, Nos. 8–9), p. 49–63.

"West Africans at Strasbourg." *West Africa,* July 1, 1961 (No. 2300), p. 707.

French Community

Ashcroft, E. W. "Towards 'Le Commonwealth.' " *West Africa,* January 9, 1960 (No. 2223), p. 39.

Crabbé, Raoul. "De l'Union Française de 1946 à la Communauté." *Eurafrica,* June 1961 (5th Year, No. 5), p. 18–21.

———. "Un Marché Commun Equatorial." *Eurafrica,* July 1961 (5th Year, No. 6), p. 25–33.

"French Community Celebrates." *West Africa,* June 25, 1960 (No. 2247), p. 711.

Hodgkin, Thomas and Ruth Schachter. "French-Speaking West Africa in Transition." *International Conciliation,* May 1960 (No. 528), p. 375–436.

"Keeping Up with the Malis." *The Economist,* June 11, 1960 (Vol. 195, No. 6094), p. 1084.

"Outlook for Africa." *The Economist,* January 29, 1961 (Vol. 198, No. 6127), p. 334.

"Overseas France." *International Developments,* January 1961 (Vol. 11, No. 1), p. 5–9.

"Plain Words for the New Community." *West Africa,* June 11, 1960 (No. 2245), p. 655.

"Plus c'a change." *West Africa,* July 16, 1960 (No. 2250), p. 786.

"Post Colonial Reunion." *The Economist,* May 28, 1960 (Vol. 195, No. 6092), p. 852.

Quermenne, J. L. "Les nouvelles institutions politiques des états d'expression française." *Civilisations,* 1961 (Vol. 11, No. 2), p. 171–186.

Rigotard, Jean. "De l'Union Française à la Communauté." *Revue d'Economie Politique,* July–October 1959 (69th Year), p. 477–540.

"Stresses in the Community." *West Africa,* September 10, 1960 (No. 2258), p. 1015.

"The Other Commonwealth." *The Economist,* May 7, 1960 (Vol. 195, No. 6089), p. 506–507.

"The Second Community." *The Economist,* August 6, 1960 (Vol. 196, No. 6102), p. 538–540.

Thompson, Virginia McLean and Richard Asloff. *The Emerging States of French Equatorial Africa.* Stanford, California, Stanford University Press, 1960. xii + 595 p.

IV. TECHNICAL ASSISTANCE AND ECONOMIC DEVELOPMENT
General

"Africa, New-Found Land." *The Economist,* September 17, 1960 (Vol. 196, No. 6108), p. 1077–1078.

Allardt, Helmut. "Praktische Möglichkeiten der Entwicklungshilfe in Africa." *Europa Archiv*, July 25, 1961 (Vol. 16, No. 14), p. 391–404.

"An Idea for Africa." *The Economist*, February 25, 1961 (Vol. 198, No. 6131), p. 677.

Benveniste, Guy and William E. Moran, Jr. *African Development—A Test for International Cooperation.* Menlo Park California, Stanford Research Institute, 1960. ix + 170 p.

Berg, Elliot J. "Economics of Independence." *West Africa*, March 10, 1962 (No. 2336), p. 255.

Bots, Maurice. " 'L'Euraficanisation' est un Marché." *Eurafrica*, November 1961 (5th Year, No. 10), p. 24–25.

Buchanan, Keith M. "The Emergence of Black Africa." *Eastern Horizon*, June 1961 (Vol. 1, No. 12), p. 11–17.

Comte, Gilbert. "Faut-il toujours aider l'Afrique?" *Communauté France-Eurafrique*, November 1961 (13th Year, No. 126), p. 17–20.

d'Arboussier, Gabriel. "La coopération des états africaines et les problèmes internationaux." *Afrique Documents*, March–April 1961 (No. 56), p. 68.

"Does Africa Need 'Aid?' " *West Africa*, December 31, 1960 (No. 2274), p. 1475.

Economic and Social Development. UN Document E/CN.14/95, January 20, 1961. 10 p.

Economic Developments in Africa, 1956–1957. UN Document E/3117, 1958 (Supplement to *World Economic Survey, 1957*). viii + 84 p.

"Economic Planning in East Africa." *African World*, March 1960, p. 6.

Economic Survey of Africa Since 1950. UN Document E/CN.14/28, 1959. xi + 248 p.

"Equipping the New Africa." *The Round Table*, December 1961 (No. 205), p. 29–36.

Europe and Africa. Forward by Per Federspeil. Strasbourg, Council of Europe, 1960. 37 p.

Fontaineau, Pierre. "Les possibilités de développement économique des pays d'Afrique." *Le Développement Africain*, May 1961 (4th Year, Special Number), p. 5–9.

Gerard, J. "Comment l'Occident peut-il aider l'Afrique?" *Eurafrica*, November 1961 (5th Year, No. 10), p. 26–27.

Guillabert, André. "Le vrai problème: déterminer en présence des conditions nouvelles de l'Afrique la coopération bien comprise des partenaires." *Communauté France-Eurafrique*, October 1961 (13th Year, No. 125), p. 4–5.

Hance, W. A. *African Economic Development.* New York, Harper, 1958. x + 307 p. + maps + tables.

"How Free Is Independent Africa?" *Africa Report*, March 1962 (Vol. 7, No. 3), p. 9–10, 18.

International Economic Assistance to Africa. UN Document E/CN.14/88, November 16, 1960. 35 p.

International Economic Assistance to Africa: A Review of Current Contributions. UN Document E/CN.14/23, November 12, 1959. 24 p. + appendix.

International Economic Assistance to Africa, 1960. UN Document E/CN.14/152, December 28, 1961. 53 p.

International Economic Assistance to the Less Developed Countries. [Report of the Secretary-General to ECOSOC (30th session)]. UN Document E/3395/Rev. 1, 1961. vii + 52 p.

Nkrumah, Kwame. "African Prospect." *Foreign Affairs*, October 1958 (Vol. 37, No. 1), p. 45–53.

Pedini, Mario. "Linea di una politica di collaborazione economica con l'Africa nera." *Rivista di Politica Economica*, February 1962 (52d Year, No. 2), p. 177–190.

Recent Developments in Western European Economic Groupings as Far as They Concern African Countries. UN Document E/CN.14/139 and Adds.1 and 2, November 15, 1961.

Report of the Ad Hoc Committee of Government Representatives on the Impact of Western European Economic Groupings in African Economies (Addis Ababa, 23–20 January, 1961). UN Document E/CN.14/100, February 1, 1961. 16 p.

Rivkin, Arnold. "A Proposal for Africa." *Africa Special Report*, September 1958 (Vol. 3, No. 9), p. 5–10.

———. *Africa and the West.* New York, Praeger, 1962. 220 p.

———. "Point Four in Africa." *Africa Special Report*, May 1960 (Vol. 5, No. 5), p. 11–12.

————. "The Politics of African Development External Aid." *The Economic Bulletin* (Published by the Economic Society of Ghana), November 1959 (Vol. 3, No. 11), p. 1–21.

Rostow, W. W. "African Economies, Lessons of History." *Africa Today*, Part I, November 1960 (Vol. 7, No. 7), p. 5–8; Part II, December 1960 (Vol. 7, No. 8), p. 11–13.

"Special Issue—Africa." *Technical Assistance Newsletter*, June–July 1961 (Vol. 2, No. 3). 16 p.

"The Economic Problems of Africa," in Legum, Colin, *Africa: A Handbook to the Continent.* London, Anthony Blond, Ltd., 1961; New York, Frederick A. Praeger, 1962; p. 476–487.

"The Other Communities." *The Economist*, November 19, 1960 (Vol. 197, No. 6117), p. 658–659.

"The Tubman Plan." *The Economist*, June 11, 1960 (Vol. 195, No. 6094), p. 1084.

Commission for Technical Cooperation in Africa South of the Sahara (CCTA)
Scientific Council for Africa South of the Sahara (CSA)

"Assistance in Africa." *West Africa*, February 22, 1958 (No. 2132), p. 176.

"C.C.T.A. Moves to Africa." *West Africa*, May 23, 1959 (No. 2197), p. 499.

"C.C.T.A. Meetings This Year." *West Africa*, January 2, 1960 (No. 2222), p. 25.

"Problems of African Co-operation." *West Africa*, February 11, 1961 (No. 2280), p. 147.

"Prospects for C.C.T.A." *West Africa*, March 17, 1962 (No. 2337), p. 287.

"Sierra Leone Joins C.C.T.A." *West Africa*, February 17, 1962 (No. 2333), p. 175.

"Scientists in Accra." *West Africa*, August 30, 1958 (No. 2159), p. 827.

Colonial Development Corporation (CDC)
Commonwealth Development Finance Company (CDFC)

"C.D.C. and the Cameroons." *West Africa*, March 19, 1960 (No. 2233), p. 324.

"C.D.C. and C.D.F.C." *West Africa*, June 10, 1961 (No. 2297), p. 623.

"C.D.C. in West Africa." *West Africa*, January 10, 1959 (No. 2178), p. 43.

"C.D.F.C. in Nigeria." *West Africa*, September 5, 1959 (No. 2205), p. 697.

"Financial Changes for C.D.C." *West Africa*, September 5, 1959 (No. 2205), p. 697.

"Lord Reith's Epilogue." *West Africa*, June 20, 1959 (No. 2201), p. 583.

Commonwealth Relations Office (CRO)

"Africa in London." *The Economist*, April 2, 1960 (Vol. 195, No. 6084), p. 17.

"Commonwealth Co-operation." *West Africa*, January 23, 1960 (No. 2225), p. 109.

"Commonwealth without Colonies." *West Africa*, June 18, 1960 (No. 2246), p. 673.

"C.R.O. Moves into Trouble." *West Africa*, September 10, 1960 (No. 2258), p. 1014.

"Expansion in UK Technical Aid." *West Africa*, November 18, 1961 (No. 2320), p. 1289.

"Merger in Whitehall." *The Economist*, December 24, 1960 (Vol. 197, No. 6133), p. 1302–1303.

"New C.R.O. Man." *West Africa*, July 30, 1960 (No. 2252), p. 841.

"New Nations & Development Issues—The British Contribution." *British Affairs*, Winter 1961 (Vol. 5, No. 4), p. 188–201.

"Problems of Commonwealth Co-operation." *West Africa*, June 4, 1960 (No. 2244), p. 641.

Development Assistance Group (DAG)

"DAG." *Eurafrica*, April 1961 (5th Year, No. 2), p. 29.

"Mainly a Forum." *The Economist*, April 29, 1961 (Vol. 199, No. 6140), p. 429.

"The Best and Worst of Aid." *The Economist*, March 25, 1961 (Vol. 198, No. 6135), p. 1155–1156.

EUROPEAN DEVELOPMENT FUND FOR THE OVERSEAS COUNTRIES AND TERRITORIES (EDFOCT)

"Community and the Developing Countries." *European Economic Community. 4th General Report of the Community, 16 May 1960–30 April 1961.* European Economic Community, May 1961. Chapter III, p. 165–193.

de Lattre, Jean-Michel. "An African Economic Community." *International Developments,* January 1961 (Vol. 11, No. 1), p. 22–27.

Durand-Reville, L. "Capitaux privés et développement." *Eurafrica,* March 1961 (5th Year, No. 2), p. 12–15.

Fonds Européen de Développement. "Comte rendu sur l'état d'avancement des opérations du Fonds Européen de Développement arrêté à la date du 30 Juin 1961." *Journal Officiel des Communautés Européennes,* October 4, 1961 (4th Year, No. 64), p. 1166–1188.

FOUNDATION FOR MUTUAL ASSISTANCE TO AFRICA SOUTH OF THE SAHARA (FAMA)

"F.A.M.A. and Ghana." *West Africa,* January 25, 1958 (No. 2128), p. 73.

"F.A.M.A.'s Second Year." *West Africa,* September 12, 1959 (No. 2206), p. 711.

INVESTMENT FUND FOR ECONOMIC AND SOCIAL DEVELOPMENT (FIDES)
[CURRENTLY, FUND FOR AID AND COOPERATION (FAC)]

"Africa and the French Economy." *West Africa,* November 18, 1961 (No. 2320), p. 1281.

Cornet, Claude. "Competition for France in her Overseas Territories." *International Developments,* January 1961 (Vol. 11, No. 1), p. 20–31.

Servoisé, Rene. "French Economic Aid to Africa." *International Developments,* January 1961 (Vol. 11, No. 1), p. 16–21.

ORGANIZATION FOR ECONOMIC COOPERATION AND DEVELOPMENT (OECD)
[FORMERLY ORGANIZATION FOR EUROPEAN ECONOMIC COOPERATION (OEEC)]

Economic Development of Overseas Countries and Territories Associated with OEEC Member Countries. Paris, Organization for European Economic Cooperation, 1958.

The Flow of Financial Resources to Countries in the Course of Economic Development, 1956–1959. Paris, Organization for European Economic Cooperation, 1961. 154 p.

The Flow of Financial Resources to Countries in the Course of Economic Development in 1960. Paris, Organization for Economic Cooperation and Development, 1962. 43 p.

SPECIAL COMMONWEALTH AFRICAN ECONOMIC ASSISTANCE PLAN (SCAAP)

"Plan for Africa." *West Africa,* September 24, 1960 (No. 2260), p. 1095.

UNITED NATIONS

GENERAL

Economic Bulletin for Africa, January 1961 (Vol. 1, No. 1), and June 1961 (Vol. 1, No. 2). Addis Ababa, Ethiopia, ECA Secretariat.

Information Paper on the Special Fund Activities in Africa. UN Document E/CN.14/156, January 15, 1962. 11 p.

Owen, David. "Technical Assistance in Africa," in Legum, Colin, *Africa: A Handbook to the Continent.* London, Anthony Blond, Ltd., 1961; New York, Frederick A. Praeger, 1962; p. 500–504.

Structure and Growth of Selected African Economies. UN Documents E/3137 and ST/ECA/57, New York, 1958. xi + 201 p.

Summary of Current Programmes of the United Nations and Specialized Agencies Relating to Africa. UN Document E/CN.14/5, November 26, 1958. 69 p. + annex.

"The Expanded Program of Technical Assistance—A Statistical Summary of Activities from July 1950–June 1961." *Technical Assistance Newsletter,* August–September 1961 (Vol. 2, No. 4). 49 p.

The United Nations and Africa—A Collection of Basic Information on the Economic and Social Activities of the United Nations and Related Agencies in Africa. UN Office of Public Information, February 1962.

United Nations Programmes for Technical Assistance in Public Administration. UN Document E/CN.14/89, November 16, 1960. 10 p.

ECONOMIC COMMISSION FOR AFRICA (ECA)

"Africa's Economic Parliament." *West Africa,* Part 1, February 27, 1960 (No. 2230), p. 245; Part 2, March 5, 1960 (No. 2231), p. 265.

Clay, George. "The Economic Commission for Africa." *West Africa,* January 24, 1959 (No. 2180), p. 81.

"Economic Commission for Africa." *West Africa,* January 3, 1959 (No. 2177), p. 19.

Economic Commission for Africa. *Annual Report (7 January 1959–6 February 1960).* ECOSOC, *Official Records* (30th session), Supplement No. 10. 42 p.

————. *Annual Report (7 February 1960–18 February 1961).* ECOSOC, *Official Records* (32d session), Supplement No. 10. 57 p.

————. *Report of the First Session (29 December 1958–6 January 1959).* ECOSOC, *Official Records* (28th session), Supplement No. 10. 22 p.

"Economic Commission Takes a Look at Africa's Development Problems." *United Nations Review,* February 1960 (Vol. 6, No. 8), p. 6–7, 31–34.

"Economists at Addis Ababa." *West Africa,* Part 1, February 18, 1961 (No. 2281), p. 184; Part 2, February 25, 1961 (No. 2282), p. 199.

"Economists in Addis Ababa." *West Africa,* March 17, 1962 (No. 2337), p. 283.

"Europe and Africa—by E.C.A." *West Africa,* March 25, 1961 (No. 2286), p. 315.

Hoffman, Paul H. "The Economic Commission for Africa," in Legum, Colin, *Africa: A Handbook to the Continent.* London, Anthony Blond, Ltd., 1961; New York, Frederick A. Praeger, 1962; p. 488–490.

"U.N. Economic Commission for Africa." *West Africa,* May 24, 1958 (No. 2145), p. 501.

"UN Economic Commission for Africa: A Report of the First Meeting." *Africa Special Report,* March 1959 (Vol. 4, No. 3), p. 13–14.

Weiss, Peter. "Making Up for Lost Time: A Report on the Economic Commission for Africa." *Africa Today,* May 1960 (Vol. 7, No. 3), p. 9–10.

SPECIALIZED AGENCIES

Food and Agriculture Organization (FAO)

The Food and Agriculture Situation in Africa. UN Document E/CN.14/166, November 15, 1961. 16 p.

International Bank for Reconstruction and Development

"Development on the Agenda." *West Africa,* October 24, 1959 (No. 2212), p. 873.

"Germany and World Bank Study Tanganyika Development." *Africa Report,* April 1961 (Vol. 6, No. 4), p. 12.

Kamarck, Andrew M. "The Activities of the World Bank in Africa," in Legum, Colin, *Africa: A Handbook to the Continent.* London, Anthony Blond, Ltd., 1961; New York, Frederick A. Praeger, 1962; p. 505–507.

"Kenya Land Settlement Program Assisted by World Bank Loan." *Africa Report,* January 1962 (Vol. 7, No. 1), p. 6.

"Sudan's Roseires Dam Project Receives World Bank Support." *Africa Report,* July 1961 (Vol. 6, No. 7), p. 7.

Technical Assistance Activities of the International Bank for Reconstruction and Development in Africa. UN Document E/CN.14/135, December 15, 1961. 4 p.

The World Bank in Africa—A Summary of Activities. Washington, D.C., International Bank for Reconstruction and Development, July 1961. 70 p.

"World Bank Lends Over Half Billion Dollars for African Development in Past Eight Years." *Africa Special Report*, July 1958 (Vol. 3, No. 7), p. 8–9.
"World Bank Loan for Nigerian Railways Sparks New Talk of Transcontinental Line." *Africa Special Report*, June 1958 (Vol. 3, No. 6), p. 13–14.
"World Bank's African Department." *West Africa*, February 10, 1962 (No. 2332), p. 163.

International Civil Aviation Organization (ICAO)

Technical Assistance Activities of the International Civil Aviation Organization in Africa. UN Document E/CN.14/160, February 26, 1962. 3 p.

International Labor Organization (ILO)

"ILO Takes Action Against South Africa." *Africa Report*, July 1961 (Vol. 6, No. 7), p. 11.
International Labor Organization. *First African Regional Conference, Lagos, December 1960. Record of Proceedings.* Geneva, International Labor Office, 1961. xxv + 310 p.
———. *First African Regional Conference, Lagos, December 1960. Report of the Director-General.* Geneva, International Labor Office, 1960. 90 p.
"International Labour in Lagos." *West Africa*, December 17, 1960 (No. 2272), p. 1415.
"The ILO in Africa." *West Africa*, January 2, 1960 (No. 2222), p. 2.

International Telecommunications Union (ITU)

Technical Assistance to the African Countries by the International Telecommunications Union. UN Document E/CN.14/106, February 9, 1961. 3 p. + annex.

United Nations Educational, Scientific, and Cultural Organization (UNESCO)

"Africans in Paris." *West Africa*, December 17, 1960 (No. 2272), p. 1437.
Final Report of the Conference of African States on the Development of Education in Africa, Addis Ababa, 15–25 May 1961. Paris, UNESCO, 1961. 127 p.
UNESCO. *Conference of African States on the Development of Education in Africa, Addis Ababa, May 15–25, 1961. Final Report.* Document UNESCO/ED/181. vi + 127 p. + addendum.
———. *Conference of African States on the Development of Education in Africa, Addis Ababa, May 15–25, 1961. Outline of a Plan for African Educational Development.* Document UNESCO/ED/180. 27 p.
"UNESCO Conference Discusses Press." *Africa Report*, February 1962 (Vol. 7, No. 2), p. 18.

World Health Organization (WHO)

"Health in Africa." *World Health Chronicle*, October 1960 (Vol. 14, No. 10), p. 394–399.
"W.H.O. Work in Africa." *West Africa*, December 6, 1958 (No. 2173), p. 1155.
World Health Organization—International Assistance Activities in Africa. UN Document E/CN.14/131, January 10, 1962. 5 p.

World Meteorological Organization (WMO)

World Meteorological Organization Technical Assistance Activities In Africa. UN Document E/CN.14/105, February 9, 1960. 3 p. + annex.

V. AFRICAN TRADE UNION MOVEMENTS

General

"Africa Labor at the Crossroads." *Africa Report*, August 1961 (Vol. 6, No. 8), p. 5.
Friedland, William H. "Decision-Making in Africa: A Case Study." *Africa Today*, December 1961 (Vol. 8, No. 10), p. 14–15.
Hoskyns, Catherine. "African Unions and Politics." *West Africa*, Part I, September 3, 1960 (No. 2257), p. 987; Part 2, September 10, 1960 (No. 2258), p. 1028.

Roberts, Margaret. "African Trade Unionism in Transition." *The World Today*, October 1961 (Vol. 17, No. 10), p. 447–455.

Satterthwaite, Joseph C. "Labor in Africa: An American Appraisal." *Africa Special Report*, April 1959 (Vol. 4, No. 4), p. 11–13.

AFRICAN TRADE UNION CONFEDERATION (ATUC)

"Confermata a Dakar: La crisi sindicale africana." *Relazioni Internazionali*, January 27, 1962 (26th Year, No. 4), p. 92.

"56 Trade Unions at Dakar." *West Africa*, January 13, 1962 (No. 2328), p. 39.

"New Trade Union Group Established at Dakar." *Africa Report*, February 1962 (Vol. 7, No. 2), p. 15.

"Pan-African Trade Unionists." *West Africa*, January 20, 1962 (No. 2329), p. 67.

Rolland, Max. "La Confédération Syndicale Africaine créée à Dakar par les délégues de trente pays." *Communauté France-Eurafrique*, December 1961—January 1962 (13th Year, No. 127), p. 11–13.

ALL-AFRICAN TRADE UNION FEDERATION (AATUF)

"All-Africa Trade Union." *West Africa*, October 17, 1959 (No. 2211), p. 863.

"All-African Trade Union Squabbles." *West Africa*, June 10, 1961 (No. 2297), p. 639.

Gordon, Roland. "African Labor Disunity." *New Leader*, July 3–10, 1961 (Vol. 44, No. 27), p. 10–11.

Marinović, M. "Realization of the Conception of African Workers' Unity—Foundation of All-African Trade Union Federation." *Review of International Affairs* (Yugoslav), July 5–20, 1961 (Vol 12, Nos. 270–271), p. 19–21.

"The People's Two Voices." *West Africa*, November 28, 1959 (No. 2217), p. 1015.

"Unions and Pan-Africa." *West Africa*, June 3, 1961 (No. 2296), p. 603.

"Uniting the World's Workers." *West Africa*, June 17, 1961 (No. 2298), p. 657.

Young, Gavin. "African Voices at Tunis." *West Africa*, February 13, 1960 (No. 2228), p. 177.

INTERNATIONAL CONFEDERATION OF FREE TRADE UNIONS (ICFTU)

"ICFTU Allows Autonomy for African Unions." *Africa Special Report*, December 1959 (Vol. 4, No. 12), p. 6–7.

"I.C.F.T.U. in Africa." *Venture*, February 1961 (Vol. 31, No. 2), p. 5.

"I.C.F.T.U. Regional Organization in Africa." *West Africa*, December 19, 1959 (No. 2220), p. 1121.

"Labor Group Reaffirms Its Ties with ICFTU." *Africa Special Report*, November 1959 (Vol. 4, No. 11), p. 5.

"Northern Cameroons Surprise." *West Africa*, November 14, 1959 (No. 2215), p. 975.

VI. AFRICAN CONFERENCE ON THE RULE OF LAW (LAGOS)

African Conference on the Rule of Law, Lagos, Nigeria, January 3–7, 1961: A Report on the Proceedings of the Conference. Geneva, International Commission of Jurists, 1961. 181 p.

Frank, Thomas M. "Out of Lagos Shall Go Forth the Law." *Africa Today*, February 1961 (Vol. 8, No. 2), p. 4, 11.

"Lagos Resolutions." *West Africa*, January 21, 1961 (No. 2277), p. 63.

"The Law of Lagos." *West Africa*, January 21, 1961 (No. 2277), p. 72.

CONTRIBUTORS

RUPERT EMERSON is Professor of Government and Research Associate at the Center for International Affairs at Harvard University and a member of the Board of Editors of *International Organization*. He is the author of several books, including *From Empire to Nation*.

PAUL-MARC HENRY is the former Secretary-General of the Commission for Technical Cooperation in Africa South of the Sahara (CCTA) and the Scientific Council for Africa South of the Sahara (CSA). He is currently Associate Director of Operations of the U.N. Special Fund.

STANLEY HOFFMANN is Associate Professor of Government at Harvard University, a member of the Board of Editors of *International Organization*, and the editor of *Contemporary Theory in International Relations*.

JOHN HOLMES is President of the Canadian Institute of International Affairs. He was for some time in the Canadian Foreign Service and, during the preparation of this essay, attended the Commonwealth Relations Conference in Lagos, Nigeria.

ERASMUS H. KLOMAN, Jr., is in the Office of the Chairman, American Metal Climax, Inc., New York. This study was made while he served as Assistant to the Director of the Foreign Policy Research Institute of the University of Pennsylvania. From 1950 until 1953, he was Special Assistant to the Assistant Secretary of State for Public Affairs.

NORMAN J. PADELFORD is Professor of Political Science and a member of the Senior Staff of the Center for International Studies at the Massachusetts Institute of Technology. Chairman of the Board of Editors of *International Organization*, he is the co-author of *The Dynamics of International Politics*.

JOHN H. SPENCER is Professor of International Law and Diplomacy at the Fletcher School of Law and Diplomacy. From 1943 until 1961, he was Senior Adviser in Foreign Affairs to the Ethiopian Government.